Stand
Perfect in
Wisdom

Stand Perfect in Wisdom

An Exposition of Colossians and Philemon

ROBERT G. GROMACKI

BAKER BOOK HOUSE
Grand Rapids, Michigan 49506

Copyright 1981 by
Baker Book House Company
ISBN 0-8010-3767-0

First printing, July 1981
Second printing, November 1982

PHOTOLITHOPRINTED BY CUSHING - MALLOY, INC.
ANN ARBOR, MICHIGAN, UNITED STATES OF AMERICA

To my
daughter-in-law
Kim Henderson Gromacki

Contents

Preface

Two enemies of the evangelical church today are intellectualism and legalism. The former exalts the mind to the exclusion of the heart, whereas the latter stresses outward conformity rather than inward transformation. Gnosticism elevates knowledge above faith, while ecclesiastical traditionalism suppresses grace with laws. In most situations, these errors are found separately; however, they were joined in the heresy which affected the church at Colosse. Paul attacked these two errors through the exposition of true spiritual wisdom and of the believer's positional completeness in Christ. In studying Colossians, therefore, you will see how a submissive life of faith and grace is the only spiritual experience which will glorify Christ.

This study has been designed to teach the Word of God to others. It is an attempt to make clear the meaning of the English text (King James Version) through organization, exposition, and careful usage of the Greek text. It is planned as a readable study, using a nontechnical vocabulary and smooth transitions from one section to the next. The words of the English text are denoted by quotation marks for easy reference, the Greek words are transliterated, and necessary grammatical explanations have been put into the footnotes.

Divided into thirteen chapters, this book can be used by adult Sunday-school classes or Bible-study groups for a traditional quarter of thirteen weeks. Concluding each chapter are discussion questions, designed to stimulate personal inquiry and to make the truth of God relevant. This book can also be used as a private Bible-study guide. In either case, this study should be read with an open Bible. It is my prayer that men and women will be blessed and edified as they undertake this study of Colossians and Philemon.

A special word of thanks is extended to Cornelius Zylstra and Dan Van't Kerkhoff, editors of Baker Book House, who encouraged and assisted me in this project. This volume will complement my other expositions: *Called to be Saints* (I Corinthians); *Stand Firm in the Faith* (II Corinthians); *Stand Fast in Liberty* (Galatians); and *Stand United in Joy* (Philippians)

Also, my love and appreciation go to my wife, Gloria, and to my daughter, Gail, who both carefully typed the manuscript.

Part 1
Colossians

Introduction

I. WRITER

All evidence definitely points to Paul as the author. He called himself by name three times (1:1, 23; 4:18). He identified himself both as an apostle and a minister (1:1, 23, 25). He ended the epistle with his typical handwritten salutation (4:18; cf. II Thess. 3:17). His associates who were with him when he wrote the epistle (1:1; 4:9–14) are also mentioned in Philemon (1, 10, 23–24): Timothy, Onesimus, Aristarchus, Mark, Epaphras, Luke, and Demas. In both of these books, he addressed Archippus (Col. 4:17; Philem. 2). These features argue for a single author of both books at the same time and place.

Some people have argued against Pauline authorship by stating that the style and vocabulary in this book are different from the style and vocabulary in his other epistles. The nature of the subject matter often determines the literary style and the choice of words, however. Actually, the content of Ephesians and Colossians is similar. Others feel that the nature of the heresy was too advanced for the sixth and seventh decades of the first century and that it reflects a second-century error; however, the book refutes an incipient Gnosticism, not a mature expression. Some critics believe that the theological concepts of Christ's person and work are also advanced, but His sovereign deity is expressed elsewhere by Paul (cf. Phil. 2:5–11).

II. CITY OF COLOSSE

The city was situated on a rocky ridge overlooking the valley of the Lycus River that runs through this mountainous district. Colosse was located about one hundred miles east of Ephesus and about eleven miles east and slightly south of Laodicea.

In the fifth century B.C., during the Persian wars, Colosse was an important city, but as her companion cities Laodicea and Hierapolis grew, she declined. In New Testament times she was less important than the other two. However, the city did retain some mercantile value because it was one of the stops on the trade route to the East and because glossy black wool was provided through the sheep industry in adjoining hills.

The city was destroyed by an earthquake during the reign of Nero, but it was quickly rebuilt. Today, the ancient site lies in ruins with a modern town, Chronas, located nearby.

III. ESTABLISHMENT OF THE CHURCH

The evangelization of Colosse is not specifically mentioned in the Book of Acts. During Paul's three years of ministry in Ephesus, Luke recorded "that all they which dwelt in Asia heard the word of the Lord Jesus, both Jews and Greeks" (Acts 19:10). Most scholars think that it was at this time the church at Colosse was founded.

Paul, though, probably did not go to Colosse himself. He wrote: "For I would that ye knew what great conflict I have for you, and for them at Laodicea, and for as many as have not seen my face in the flesh" (2:1). This verse suggests that both the Laodicean and the Colossian churches had not experienced his direct, personal ministry.

How then were the churches started? There are two plausible alternatives. The first is that one of Paul's associates, possibly Timothy, went into the region of Laodicea and Colosse during the apostle's stay at Ephesus. Perhaps this is why the name of Timothy is included in the introductory greeting (1:1). The second is that residents of Laodicea and Colosse, perhaps Epaphras (1:7–8; 4:12–13), Nymphas (4:15), and/or Philemon (Philem. 1–2), journeyed to Ephesus, were saved directly through Paul's ministry, returned to their hometowns, and started churches there. Since Paul had led Philemon to Christ (Philem. 19) and knew several by name in Colosse and Laodicea (Epaphras, Nymphas, Philemon, Apphia, and Archippus), this view looms as the more likely possibility. The converts of these initial converts never had had the privilege of seeing Paul, and yet they looked to him for apostolic direction. In a sense, he was their spiritual grandfather. This is why Paul's knowledge of their spiritual condition was secondhand (1:4, 8).

The membership was composed largely, if not exclusively, of Gentiles. Paul identified them as "being dead in your sins and the uncircumcision of your flesh" (2:13; cf. Eph. 2:1). "Uncircumcision" is a designation for Gentiles (cf. Rom. 2:24–27; Eph. 2:11). It is possible that the phrases "among the Gentiles" and "in you" were meant to be synonymous (1:27). The phrase, "And you, that were sometimes alienated and enemies in your mind" (1:21), sounds like Paul's description of lost Gentiles elsewhere (Eph. 2:11–12; 4:17–18).

IV. NATURE OF THE HERESY

The false teaching at Colosse consisted of a mixture or merger of Jewish legalism, Greek or incipient Gnostic philosophy, and possibly Oriental mysticism. Because of these diverse elements, some scholars have thought that Paul was dealing with two or three different groups of false teachers; however, as a study of the book shows, the characteristics are so interwoven as to suggest one group of heretics with multiple errors in their teaching.

Were these teachers Jewish or Gentile? It is difficult to say with certainty; neither answer affects the content of the heresy. Thus it is safe to identify the false teaching as either Judaistic Gnosticism or Gnostic Judaism.

Many Jews lived in that area because their ancestors were forced to migrate there under the Seleucid ruler, Antiochus III. The descendants eventually strayed away from orthodox Judaism and succumbed to the influence of Greek philosophy. The heresy at Colosse did have a strong Jewish ritualistic character, whereas second-century Gnosticism manifested more the philosophical element.

It is also difficult to determine whether these heretics were within the church membership or attacked the church from without. Paul warned against both sources (Acts 20:29–30). Since the church was young and did have some adequate leadership, it would seem that the heresy came as an outside threat.

What was this heresy? It taught that spiritual knowledge is available only to those with superior intellects, thus creating a spiritual caste system. Faith was treated with contempt; advanced Gnosticism even taught that salvation is received by knowledge. Adherents believed that they could understand divine mysteries totally unknown and unavailable to the typical Christian.

An influence of Greek philosophy was its teaching that all matter is innately evil and that the soul or mind is intrinsically good. This logically led to a denial of the creation of the material world by God and to a denial of the incarnation of Jesus Christ. The latter involved a repudiation of His humanity, His physical death, and His physical resurrection.

To explain the existence of the material world, the heretics taught that a series of angelic emanations created it. According to these teachers, God created an angel who created another angel who in turn created another angel *ad infinitum*. The last angel in this series then created the world. This angelic cosmogony thus denied God's direct creation and supervision of the world. This conviction resulted in some practical theological error. It stressed the transcendence of God to the exclusion of His immanence. Since God did not create the world in the past, the heretics argued, He does not work in the world in the present. This ruled out the value of prayer or the possibility of miracles. It led to a false worship of angels. If the world resulted from angelic emanations, then the person in the world had to work his way back to God through this series. Thus he would have to know who those angels were and how many there were in order to give each his proper respect.

Christ was reduced by most Gnostics into a creature, perhaps the highest being that God created. This was an attack upon the Trinity and upon the eternal, sovereign deity of Jesus Christ.

In daily living, the heresy led to asceticism and legalism. If matter is evil, then the body is evil. The heresy taught that to destroy the desires of the body (in order to satisfy the needs of the soul), a rigid code of behavior—including circumcision, dietary laws, and observances of feasts—had to be followed.

INTRODUCTION

V. TIME AND PLACE

During Paul's absence from Asia, this heresy began to infiltrate the area. The leaders of the Colossian church were apparently unable to cope with it, so they sent Epaphras to Rome to consult with Paul. Quite possibly, Epaphras was the founder and pastor of the church. When he left, Archippus assumed the pastoral responsibility (1:7; 4:17). Epaphras informed Paul of the Colossians' faith (1:4–5), their love for Paul (1:8), and the heretical threat.

Unable to go to Colosse because of his imprisonment, Paul penned this epistle and sent it to the church through Tychicus and Onesimus (4:7–9). For some unknown reason, Epaphras was imprisoned along with Paul by the Roman government (Philem. 23). Since Epaphras could not return to Colosse at this time to correct the situation with the apostolic authority of the epistle, the task was assigned to Tychicus. However, Paul assured the church members that Epaphras was laboring "fervently for [them] in prayers, that [they] may stand perfect and complete in all the will of God" (4:12). Thus, within eight years of the establishment of the church, Paul had to write to this young, immature, threatened church to warn it against the errors of the heresy (2:8, 16, 20).

VI. PURPOSES

Paul wrote, therefore, to express his prayerful interest in the spiritual development of the Colossian believers (1:1–12), to set forth the sovereign headship of Jesus Christ over creation and the church (1:13–29), to warn against the moral and doctrinal errors of the heresy (2:1–23), to exhort the Colossians to a life of holiness (3:1—4:6), to explain the mission of Tychicus and Onesimus (4:7–9), to send greetings from his associates (4:10–15), and to command the exchange of correspondence with the Laodicean church (4:16–18).

VII. DISTINCTIVE FEATURES

The epistle's close resemblance to Ephesians both in content and vocabulary must be mentioned. So much of Colossians is repeated in Ephesians that the two books must have been written at the same time and place. Here are some related contrasts:

Colossians	Ephesians
Completeness in Christ	Oneness in Christ
Mystery of Christ in the body of the believer	Mystery of Jews and Gentiles as one in the body of Christ
Emphasis on Christ as the head of the body	Emphasis on the church as the body of Christ

Colossians contains a classic passage on the preeminence of Jesus Christ (1:14–22). This passage actually develops grammatically as a relative clause ("in whom," *en hōi*) within the apostle's prayer (1:9–14). The listed descriptive titles of Christ are unique: the image of the invisible God, the first-born of every creature, the head of the body, the beginning, and the first-born from the dead. His role as creator of the universe is explained through four prepositional phrases: sphere of creation (literally, "in him," *en autōi;* 1:16); agent of creation ("by him," *di' autou;* 1:16); goal of creation ("for him," *eis auton;* 1:16); and prior to creation ("before all things," *pro pantōn;* 1:17). Paul also called Him the sustainer of creation ("by him all things consist," 1:17). Both in the natural and in the spiritual creations, Christ is sovereign and should have the preeminence.

Colossians contains the most severe warning against unguided human intellect or nonbiblical philosophy: "Beware lest any man spoil you through philosophy and vain deceit, after the tradition of men, after the rudiments of the world, and not after Christ" (2:8). The Greek word for "philosophy" *(philosophia)* means "love of wisdom." In Christ are "hid all the treasures of wisdom *[sophias]* and knowledge" (2:3); therefore, a genuine love for wisdom should lead to a perfect love for Christ. However, many systems that exist under the guise of philosophy are really governed by human or world standards, by humanism or antisupernaturalism, rather than by divine revelation centered in the person of Christ. Christians need to distinguish between true and false philosophies.

1

The Important Positions
Colossians 1:1–2

What do you write to a church located in a city which you have never visited? How do you introduce yourself? How do you describe your readers?

This was not the first time that Paul encountered this situation in his writing ministry. He had written the Epistle to the Romans in anticipation of later making an initial visit to that main city of the imperial government. In that letter, however, he sent greetings to many friends who had migrated to Rome; thus, the people of that church were not entirely unknown to him (Rom. 16:3–15).

Contrariwise, both the church and the city of Colosse were unknown to the apostle (2:1). His travels had not taken him to that city and he knew only a few by face and by name: Epaphras (4:12), Onesimus (4:9), Philemon, Apphia, and Archippus (Philem. 1–2).

In spite of this personal unfamiliarity, the epistle manifests a loving bond of spiritual oneness in Christ. The apostle and the church members were brothers in Him.

The opening words of the letter thus set the tone for the inspired explanations and exhortations which follow. They establish the stance from which Paul will speak to the Colossians and reveal his assessment of their spiritual position.

I. THE SALUTATION (1:1–2a)

The introductory remarks contain what is normally found within a Pauline greeting: description of self, associate, and readers; a blessing; and a prayer of thanksgiving (cf. Rom. 1:1–8; Phil. 1:1–7; I Thess. 1:1–2; II Thess. 1:1–3).

A. Author (1:1)

1. His name

Born into the Jewish tribe of Benjamin, Paul was probably named by his parents after the first king of Israel (Phil. 3:5; cf. I Sam. 9:1–2). In his pre-Christian life, he was known as Saul of Tarsus, the persecutor of the church (Acts 7:58; 8:1, 3; 9:1). When Christ revealed Himself to the young Pharisee, He addressed him as Saul (Acts 9:4). For the next nine years of Paul's Christian life, he maintained the usage of that given name (Acts 9:17, 19, 22, 26; 11:25, 30; 13:1–2).

Since persons born into bilingual countries were often given two names, some commentators have conjectured that he also received the name Paul *(Paulos)* at birth. It is true that he came from a Jewish family which possessed Roman citizenship and which lived in Tarsus, the chief city of Cilicia and one of the great learning centers of the Eastern world.

A more plausible explanation is that he changed his name from Saul to Paul at the beginning of his first missionary journey (Acts 13:9, 13). On this occasion, at Cyprus, he demonstrated his apostolic authority for the first time by imposing blindness upon the sorcerer Elymas, who had resisted the gospel witness. Through this miracle, he won his first convert, the Roman proconsul Sergius Paulus (Acts 13:7–12). It is reasonable to conclude that he assumed this man's name as a constant reminder of the grace and power of God who can save sinners and call them into Christian service.[1] Otherwise, it would be a mere coincidence that Luke recorded the change in the apostle's name in the midst of this narrative detailing the salvation experience of the Roman deputy.

The Latin *paulus* actually means "little" or "small." The English noun *pauper* is derived from it. In a true spiritual analogy, Paul

---

[1] Two early church fathers, Jerome and Augustine, both believed that Paul took his new name from Sergius Paulus.

saw himself as "the least of all saints" (Eph. 3:8). Even late in life, he still viewed himself as the "chief" of sinners (I Tim. 1:15). This new name manifested the change from the pride of Phariseeism to the humility of Christianity. His namesake, King Saul, who was physically tall, was humbled by God because of pride and arrogant self-will. The self-assured religious bigot was also humbled by God on the road to Damascus, but he arose to become a dedicated servant of Christ.

A man is known by his name, and Paul epitomized his.

2. His life

What can be said about this amazing life? Almost the entire history of the apostolic church can be equated with the personal history of Paul, the greatest of the apostles.

Because Paul's parents were Jews who possessed Roman citizenship, he inherited a unique status: he was both a Jew and a Roman (Acts 22:25–29). His Jewish heritage was flawless: "Circumcised the eighth day, of the stock of Israel, of the tribe of Benjamin, an Hebrew of the Hebrews" (Phil. 3:5). As did other Jewish male children, he learned a manual trade; in his case, tentmaking (Acts 18:3). Probably at the age of thirteen, he was sent by his wealthy, Pharisaic father to study in Jerusalem under the learned and respected Gamaliel, also a Pharisee and a doctor of the Mosaic law (Acts 5:34–39; 22:3; 23:6). In those years of training, he "profited in the Jews' religion above many [his] equals in [his] own nation, being more exceedingly zealous of the traditions of [his] fathers" (Gal. 1:14). Within his peer group, he showed the most promise of becoming an outstanding Pharisee.

Paul was first mentioned in Scripture as the young man in charge of the robes of those who stoned Stephen (Acts 7:58). From that point on, he became a fanatical persecutor of Christians, both imprisoning them and putting them to death (Acts 22:4; 26:10–11; Gal. 1:13). Christians everywhere were deathly afraid of him (Acts 9:13, 26). If judged by his attitudes and actions, Saul of Tarsus must have been considered the most unlikely candidate for salvation, and yet God sovereignly saved him when Jesus Christ manifested Himself to him on the road to Damascus (I Tim. 1:12–16; cf. Acts 9:1–16; Gal. 1:11–15; A.D. 32). Through this supernatural revelation and others, Paul became both a witness of the resurrected Christ and a commissioned apostle (Acts 9:15–16; I Cor. 15:8–10).

His early years of witness were spent mainly in Syria, Arabia, and Judea (Acts 9:19–29; Gal. 1:17–22; A.D. 32–35). He then went into relative seclusion at his hometown of Tarsus for about nine years (Acts 9:30; A.D. 35–44). Barnabus brought him from Tarsus to Antioch in Syria to work in that growing church as a teacher (Acts 11:25–30; 12:25; A.D. 44–47).

Antioch then became the base for his three famous missionary journeys. His first trip took him to Seleucia, Cyprus, Perga, Pisidian Antioch, Iconium, Lystra, and Derbe (Acts 13:1—14:28; A.D. 47–48). During the second, he traveled to Syria, Cilicia, Derbe, Lystra, Phrygia, Galatia, Mysia, Troas, Philippi, Thessalonica, Berea, Athens, Corinth, Ephesus, Caesarea, and Jerusalem (Acts 18:23—21:17; A.D. 52–56).

Paul was arrested and imprisoned at Jerusalem and later at Caesarea for two years (Acts 21:18—26:32; A.D. 56–58). After a treacherous voyage, he arrived at Rome, where he remained a prisoner for two more years (Acts 27:1—28:31; A.D. 58–61). He then was released, enabling him to resume a limited itinerary, including Crete, Ephesus, and Macedonia (I Tim. 1:3; Titus 1:5; A.D. 61–64). When the imperial persecution against Christianity began during Nero's reign, Paul was arrested and taken to Rome, where he was again imprisoned (A.D. 64–67). Tradition states that he was beheaded about A.D. 67 in Rome and that his corpse was buried in the subterranean labyrinths.

3. His position

Throughout the centuries of biblical history, the authority of God's official spokesmen has been questioned. The exclusive leadership of Moses was doubted even by Miriam and Aaron, his own sister and brother (Num. 12:1–2). The priests and Levites rejected the credentials of John the Baptist (John 1:19–25). Even Jesus Christ was asked by His religious critics: "By what authority doest thou these things? and who gave thee this authority?" (Matt. 21:23).

To a church which did not know him personally and which had

been impressed with false teachers, Paul had to assert his authoritative position. *First,* he claimed to be "an apostle" *(apostolos).* He employed this official title for himself several times (Rom. 1:1; I Cor. 1:1; II Cor. 1:1; Eph. 1:1; I Tim. 1:1; II Tim. 1:1; Titus 1:1). Apostles were those believers who had seen the resurrected Christ and who had been commanded directly by Him to preach and lay the foundation for the church age (Eph. 2:20).[2] Their ministries were authenticated by miracles (Mark 16:17, 20; Heb. 2:3–4). To all churches Paul could honestly say: "Truly the signs of an apostle were wrought among you in all patience, in signs, and wonders, and mighty deeds" (II Cor. 12:12). He debated with logical, rhetorical questions: "Am I not an apostle? am I not free? have I not seen Jesus Christ our Lord? are not ye my work in the Lord?" (I Cor. 9:1). There can be no doubt that Paul was what he claimed to be. Actually, few men qualified for this rare apostolic position: the Twelve, Matthias (Acts 1:26), Barnabas (Acts 14:14), James the Lord's brother (Gal. 1:19), and Paul.[3]

Second, Paul was an apostle "of Jesus Christ." Christ both saved him and sent him forth.[4] On the occasion of his conversion, the Savior said: "But rise, and stand upon thy feet: for I have appeared unto thee for this purpose, to make thee a minister and a witness both of these things which thou hast seen, and of those things in the which I will appear unto thee" (Acts 26:16). Paul knew that he had seen the resurrected Christ and that he had been directly commissioned by Him (I Cor. 9:1; 15:8–10). The others became apostles during the Lord's earthly and preascension ministries, but Paul received that office through a unique, postascension appearance. His apostleship, nevertheless, was recognized as genuine by the Jerusalem apostles (Gal. 2:1–10).

[2] The Greek word *apostolos,* translated "apostle," comes from the verb *apostellō,* which means "to send away with a commission to do something." The original twelve apostles were selected from among many disciples to be with Christ and to be sent forth by Him to preach, heal, and cast out demons within Israel (Matt. 10:5–8; Mark 3:13–15). Excluding Judas Iscariot, this group was later recommissioned by the resurrected Christ to preach the gospel throughout the world (Matt. 28:16–20).

[3] It may be that Barnabas was an apostle in a nontechnical sense in that he was sent by the church at Antioch, but not directly by Christ.

[4] The name "Jesus Christ" thus is seen as a subjective genitive.

Third, Paul became an apostle "by the will of God" (cf. Rom. 15:32; I Cor. 1:1; II Cor. 1:1; Eph. 1:1; II Tim. 1:1). This was by God's sovereign, efficacious decree. H. C. G. Moule remarked that "with God to will implies the provision of the means of fulfillment."[5] Elsewhere, Paul wrote that "it pleased God, who separated me from my mother's womb, and called me by his grace, To reveal his Son in me" (Gal. 1:15–16). The Father and the Son always work in concert.

Furthermore, Paul asserted that he was an apostle "not of men, neither by man" (Gal. 1:1). The plural ("men") indicates that his position did not originate with the prophets and teachers at Antioch who sent both him and Barnabas on the first missionary journey (Acts 13:2–3) nor with the Jerusalem apostles (Gal. 2:1–10). In the interval between the ascension of Christ into heaven and the descent of the Holy Spirit on the day of Pentecost, the eleven apostles selected Matthias instead of Joseph Barsabas to be the apostolic replacement for Judas Iscariot (Acts 1:21–26). In a real sense, it could be said that Matthias was an apostle "of men."

The singular ("man") shows that no one man appointed Paul to this task. His critics could have easily charged that Ananias was responsible for Paul's conversion and call into the ministry (Acts 9:10–17). After all, the regenerated Saul received his sight and was filled with the Holy Spirit when Ananias laid his hands upon the apostle. However, Christ chose Paul before He appeared to Ananias and before Ananias contacted Paul. Also, the critics could have suggested that Barnabas was humanly responsible for Paul's ministry. It is true that Barnabas introduced Paul to the apostles at Jerusalem (Act 9:27), that Barnabas brought Paul to work in the church at Antioch (Acts 11:25–26), and that the name of Barnabas regularly preceded that of Paul (Acts 11:30; 12:25; 13:1, 2, 7; 14:12, 14). In spite of these facts, the Bible nowhere implies that Barnabas appointed Paul to the apostolic position.

4. His associate

First, Timothy's name *(Timotheos)* is based upon a combination of two Greek words, meaning "honor" *(timē)* and "God" *(theos).*

[5] H. C. G. Moule, *Studies in Colossians and Philemon,* p. 64.

He was one who honored God in his life and who in turn was honored by God. The Lord said to Eli, the judge who guided Samuel: ". . . for them that honour me I will honour" (I Sam. 2:30). Timothy personified that divine decree.

Second, Timothy's life history is rather complex. A native of Lystra, he was the son of a Greek father and a Jewish mother (Acts 16:1). In his early youth he was influenced by the godly lives of his grandmother, Lois, and his mother, Eunice (II Tim. 1:5; 3:15). Paul apparently converted him to Christ during the first missionary journey (I Tim. 1:2, 18; cf. Acts 14:6–23).[6] Because of Timothy's spiritual gifts and maturity, Paul selected him during the second journey to become an associate in the missionary enterprise (Acts 16:1–3). At that time he was circumcised and ordained (Acts 16:3; I Tim. 4:14; II Tim. 4:5).[7]

Timothy shared in the establishment of the work at Philippi, Thessalonica, and Berea (Acts 16:1—17:14). When he rejoined Paul at Athens, he was sent back to Thessalonica to continue the edification of that church (Acts 17:14–16; cf. I Thess. 3:1–2). He later returned to Corinth and assisted the apostle in the founding of that church (Acts 18:5).

The biblical record does not indicate whether Timothy traveled with Paul from Corinth to Ephesus, Caesarea, Jerusalem, Antioch, and finally back to Ephesus (Acts 18:18—19:1). However, he did work with Paul at Ephesus (Acts 19:22). Since this was the time that the entire province of Asia was evangelized (Acts 19:10), it may be that Timothy actually took part in the founding of the church at Colosse. This perhaps is the reason why Timothy is mentioned in the opening salutation.

Paul then sent Timothy into the provinces of Macedonia and Achaia to minister to the churches in those areas and to prepare the way for a proposed visit by the apostle (Acts 19:22; I Cor. 4:17; II Cor. 16:10). Before Paul left Ephesus, Timothy rejoined

[6] Paul's constant mention of Timothy as his son refers to the latter's conversion as well as to the close relationship which developed between them.

[7] The circumcision of Timothy was not a contradiction of Paul's teaching (cf. Gal. 5:2–3). He was circumcised not to gain justification but to increase his effectiveness as a witness to Jewish audiences who knew his racial background (cf. I Cor. 9:19–20).

him in that city (Rom. 16:21; II Cor. 1:1, 19). He then traveled with Paul from Ephesus to Macedonia and Achaia, back to Macedonia, and on to the province of Asia (Acts 20:1–5).

Again, the Scriptures are silent about the presence of Timothy during Paul's trip to Jerusalem, his arrest there, his two-year imprisonment at Caesarea, and his voyage to Rome (Acts 21:1—28:16). Timothy rejoined Paul at Rome in the early months of the apostle's imprisonment in that city. From Rome he may have prevented that desire from being fulfilled (Phil. 2:19–24).

After the apostle's release, Timothy journeyed with Paul to Ephesus where he was left to care for the church (I Tim. 1:3). He was not with Paul when the latter was arrested and quickly taken to Rome; however, the apostle requested that he come (II Tim. 4:9). It is difficult to say whether Timothy did go to Rome and whether he arrived before the apostle's martyrdom. If Paul wrote the letter to the Hebrews, there is some speculation that Timothy went to Rome was imprisoned, and later released (Heb. 13:23–24).[8] Tradition states that Timothy was martyred during the reign of either Domitian or Nerva.

Timothy was not only Paul's associate, but he also may have been the amanuensis who actually wrote the letter under the apostle's dictation and supervision.[9] However, it cannot be said that he was a coauthor. The epistle contains too many personal references to Paul to justify that conclusion (1:23–25, 29; 4:18). Since Paul and Timothy were "likeminded" (Phil. 2:19–22), the epistle did reflect the convictions and feelings of the young associate.

Third, Timothy is identified literally as "the brother" *(ho adelphos).* In derivation, the word means "from the same womb" *(apo* and *delphus).* He was a brother both to Paul and to the Colossians because all of them had been born of the Spirit into the family of God. The definite article "the" *(ho)* can be translated as "my" or "our" in this context, but its usage indicates that Timothy was known to both Paul and the church. Normally the apostle characterized his friend as his son in the faith (I Cor. 4:17; I Tim.

---

[8] The speculation could stand even if Hebrews were written by someone other than Paul.

[9] Paul used secretaries in the composition of his other letters (Rom. 16:22; Gal. 6:11; II Thess. 3:17).

1:2; II Tim. 1:2). Paul used the title "brother" to designate other believers: Quartus (Rom. 16:23), Sosthenes (I Cor. 1:1), Apollos (I Cor. 16:12), and an anonymous associate (II Cor. 8:18; 12:18).

B. Readers (1:2a)

Although only one group is in mind, they are characterized in four ways.

1. They were saints

The term "saints" is a synonym for Christian believers. It literally means "the set-apart ones" *(tois hagiois)*. It is an adjective which is used with noun force and which comes from a verb that is normally translated as "sanctify" *(hagiazō)*. Sinners become saints by divine, efficacious call and by fulfilling the human responsibility to call upon the name of Jesus Christ for salvation (I Cor. 1:2). To be a saint means to have an acceptable spiritual position before a holy God, not to be exceedingly holy in one's religious practice nor to be declared a saint after death.

The term "saints" embraces all four aspects of the verb "to sanctify." These aspects are the ministry of the Holy Spirit in the person's life before conversion (Gal. 1:15; II Thess. 2:13), the time of regeneration (I Cor. 1:2; 6:11; Heb. 10:14), the present cleansing and edifying ministry of the Christian by the Spirit through the Word of God (John 17:17), and the total separation from the effects of sin when the believer receives the incorruptible, immortal body (Eph. 5:26–27).

2. They were faithful brethren

The words "saints" and "brethren" do not refer to two separate groups; rather, they form a double description of the same group of readers.[10]

First, Paul regarded the Colossian believers as "brothers." Although he had never seen them, they were as dear to him as

---

[10]The Greek construction illustrates the Granville Sharp grammatical rule *(tois hagiois kai pistois adelphois).* The two nouns are joined by "and" and are introduced by a single article. Thus, one group is described in two ways.

Timothy, whom he looked upon often. The love and warmth of the family of God are not restricted by geography or race.

Second, the Colossians were "faithful" brothers. This adjective can be regarded in the active sense of "believing" or in the passive sense of "faithful" *(pistois).* More likely, it reflects the latter approach, describing the Colossians as trustful and full of faith. It would be redundant to relate the word to initial, saving faith since that presupposition would be enveloped within the terms "saints" and "brethren." The apostle knew that these believers had been saved by faith and that they were continuing in the faith (1:23). Later, he commanded them to keep on doing what they had done.

3. They were in Christ

The sphere of acceptance of any believing sinner is "in Christ." On the night before His crucifixion, the Lord Jesus revealed to the disciples the new relationships which would exist between Him and them after His redemptive death and resurrection: "At that day ye shall know that I am in my Father, and ye in me, and I in you" (John 14:20). This new position is secured by the baptism in the Holy Spirit (I Cor. 12:13). It results in a "new creature" (II Cor. 5:17). The epistles of Paul are dotted with such expressions as "in Him" or "in Christ" (Eph. 1:3). In Christ, the believer finds salvation, acceptance, redemption, forgiveness of sins, inheritance, and sealing by the Spirit of God (Eph. 1:4–14).

4. They were at Colosse

Spiritually, these believers were in Christ, but geographically they were "at Colosse." This city was located on the Lycus River in the region of Phrygia. The tributaries of this river brought a "calcareous deposit of a peculiar kind that choked up the streams and made arches and fantastic grottoes."[11] Colosse was only eleven miles away from Laodicea and thirteen miles from Hierapolis. These three cities formed an important political triangle which was later incorporated into the large Roman province of Asia.

---

[11] A. T. Robertson, *Word Pictures in the New Testament,* vol. 4, p. 473.

II. THE BLESSING (1:2b)

The typical Greek greeting employed the third person, but Paul conveyed a greater degree of intimacy by using the second person ("unto you").

A. Its Content

The content of the blessing was twofold: "grace" and "peace." The first word reflects a Greek concept, "grace" *(charis)*, whereas the second manifests a Hebrew concept, "peace" *(shalom)*. Grace always precedes peace and forms the foundation for the latter.

1. Grace

All believers are saved or "justified freely by his [God's] grace through the redemption that is in Christ Jesus" (Rom. 3:24). Their acceptable standing is maintained by divine grace (Eph. 2:8–9). The doctrine of grace reveals that God bestows blessings upon believing sinners apart from any merit within them. In addition, God supplies daily grace to meet the needs of the Christian, giving undeserved provision (John 1:16) and forgiving daily sins (Rom. 5:20). This apostolic blessing stresses daily grace. Although Paul constantly glorified the grace of God in his life and ministry, the word occurs only five times in this epistle (1:2, 6; 3:16; 4:6, 18). However, the book begins and ends with a pronouncement of the blessing of grace (1:2; 4:18).

2. Peace

When a sinner becomes a believing Christian, he gains an unalterable standing of peace *with* God, or *before* God (Rom. 5:1). This is judicial peace.

In the world, however, a Christian needs the peace *of* God for daily protection from hostile pressures upon his mind and heart (Phil. 4:7). If a believer could see that each day of his life begins and ends with divine grace and peace, then he would have joy and stability. Leon Morris stated that peace is "not simply the absence of strife, but the presence of positive blessings. It is the prosperity of the whole man, especially his spiritual prosperity."[12] Later in the epistle, the apostle appealed to the Colossians: "And let the peace of God rule in your hearts" (3:15). The word "peace" *(eirēnē)* occurs only twice in the book (1:2; 3:15).

B. Its Source

The source of this blessing is two persons within the divine Being: "God our Father" and "the Lord Jesus Christ." The single preposition "from" *(apo)* links the Father and the Son together as the common source.[13] Doubtless these gifts are mediated to the believer through the indwelling ministry of the Holy Spirit. One aspect of the fruit of the Spirit is peace (Gal. 5:22).

Questions for Discussion

1. Should parents select meaningful names for their children? Should they be biblical names?

2. How can the call to Christian service today be compared to the apostolic call of Paul?

3. In what ways can believers discern the will of God for a career choice? in selecting a spouse? for geographic location?

4. Using Timothy as an example, explain the advantages of in-service training? How can churches produce qualified ministers for this society?

5. How is the concept of sainthood abused today? How can that be corrected?

6. How can the sense of spiritual brotherhood be increased? How can racial and geographic barriers be overcome?

7. What constitutes faithfulness? What characteristics have often replaced it in the modern Christian?

[12] Leon Morris, *The First Epistle of Paul to the Corinthians*, (Grand Rapids: Eerdmans, 1958), p. 35.

[13] The deity of Jesus Christ is affirmed in this verse by the divine title *Lord* and by His union with the Father as the common source of grace and peace.

2

The Giving of Thanks
Colossians 1:3–8

Paul was in prison, the church had moral and doctrinal problems, but the apostle could still give thanks to God. He had neither self-pity nor a pessimistic outlook for the Colossian believers. He exemplified his instructions to others: "In every thing give thanks: for this is the will of God in Christ Jesus concerning you" (I Thess. 5:18). He practiced what he preached.

All of the epistles written to churches, with the exception of Galatians and II Corinthians, begin with a prayer of thanksgiving (Rom. 1:8; I Cor. 1:4; Eph. 1:16; Phil. 1:3; Col. 1:3; I Thess. 1:2; II Thess. 1:3). All of the letters addressed to individuals, with the exception of Titus, likewise start in the same way (I Tim. 1:12; II Tim. 1:3; Philem. 4). The cause of this thanksgiving was what God had done for these believers and what He was presently doing through them. Included among the specific areas of special praise were a witnessing faith (Rom. 1:8), the grace of God and spiritual enrichment (I Cor. 1:4–5), saving faith and brotherly love (Eph. 1:15), work of faith, labor of love, and patience of hope (I Thess. 1:3; II Thess. 1:3–4), and fellowship in the gospel (Phil. 1:3–8).

Three areas of emphasis can be gleaned from the apostle's expression of thanks in this section. Actually, the entire passage (1:3–8) constitutes one lengthy sentence in the Greek text.

I. FOR THE COLOSSIANS (1:3–4)

One of the dominant themes which manifests itself throughout the epistle is that of thanksgiving. It is mentioned in all four chapters of the book (1:3, 12; 2:7; 3:15, 17; 4:2). In this first reference, Paul is the person who renders thanks to God, but in the other passages, the Colossians are exhorted to exhibit that gracious spirit.

A. The Expression of Thanksgiving (1:3)

The plural verb ("we give thanks") indicates that both Paul and Timothy shared this spiritual conviction and exercise. The fact that more than one person was involved gives the expression greater impact—"in the mouth of two or three witnesses every word may be established" (Matt. 18:16).

1. Its meaning

The verb "give thanks" (*eucharistoumen*) is a compound word, based upon the adverb "well" or "good" (*eu*) and the noun "grace" (*charis*). It is also related to the word "joy" (*chara*). Thus, in general, the one who gives thanks is full of joy, expressing oral appreciation for his benefactor's generosity; and the one who gives thanks specifically to God expresses delight about the gift of grace.

Paul uses the verb form of "thanksgiving" twenty-four times (*eucharisteō*), the noun twelve times (*eucharistia*), and the adjective in its only New Testament occurrence (*eucharistos*).[1] In Colossians, the verb appears three times (1:3; 1:12; 3:17), the noun twice (2:7; 4:2), and the adjective once (3:15).

The present tense of the verb reveals Paul's and Timothy's constant gratitude for the repeated blessings bestowed directly upon them by God or indirectly through the changed lives of converts. The prison environment could not deter Paul from his priestly offering of praise to God. As it is expressed elsewhere:

By him therefore let us offer the sacrifice of praise to God continually, that is, the fruit of our lips giving thanks to his name.

[1]The Gospels contain only the verb—it occurs there eleven times; the verb occurs twice and the noun once in Acts; and the verb is used once and the noun twice in Revelation. No form is found in the general Epistles.

THE GIVING OF THANKS

But to do good and to communicate forget not: for with such sacrifices God is well pleased (Heb. 13:15–16).

Both Paul and Timothy performed this ministry well.

2. Its object

Paul and Timothy gave their thanks "to God and the Father of our Lord Jesus Christ." In the New Testament, the direction of thanksgiving is almost exclusively to God, with but three exceptions in the fifty-three cases (Luke 17:16; Acts 24:3; Rom. 16:4). God is always the source of gracious favors. James wrote: "Every good gift and every perfect gift is from above, and cometh down from the Father of lights, with whom is no variableness, neither shadow of turning" (James 1:17).

The title "Father of our Lord Jesus Christ" is unique to the New Testament. In the Old Testament, God was known as the God of the Hebrew fathers Abraham, Isaac, and Jacob; however, here He is seen as the God who has revealed Himself through His incarnate Son and through the latter's redemptive death and resurrection (cf. Rom. 15:6; II Cor. 1:3; 11:31; I Peter 1:3). This title also served to disprove the heretical claim that Jesus was a mere creature, related only to God by creation and not by eternal relationship.

God is not the God and Father of Jesus Christ in the same sense that He is the God and Father of believing sinners. When Christ was on earth, He addressed God as "Father" (John 17:1), "Holy Father" (John 17:11), and "My Father" (John 5:17). Never in His own prayers did He say, "Our Father." When the disciples asked to be taught about prayer, He said to them: "When *ye* pray, say, Our Father which art in heaven" (Luke 11:2, italics ours). In His first postresurrection appearance, He told Mary Magdalene to "go to my brethren, and say unto them, I ascend unto my Father, and your Father; and to my God, and your God" (John 20:17). Christ called them "my brethren," but He did not say "our Father" or "our God." His relationship to them as the offspring of Mary was one thing, but their relationship and His relationship to God the Father were altogether different. Even the religious critics of Christ knew that He was making a claim of a unique relationship to God, an assertion tantamount to blasphemy, in their opinion, because it suggested equality with God (John 5:17–18).

3. Its occasion

Paul thanked God during his prayers for the Colossians ("praying always for you"). This phrase does not mean that the apostle was constantly involved in a ministry of prayer, because he also was engaged in teaching, writing, counseling, sleeping, and eating. However, the phrase is ambiguous grammatically, since the adverb "always" (*pantote*) may modify either the main verb ("give thanks") or the participle ("praying"). The phrase does not necessarily mean that whenever Paul prayed, he always prayed for the Colossians, although that is a possibility. Rather, he always gave thanks for these believers whenever he prayed for them. His first response, whenever they came into his mind, was not to scold them nor to be disappointed in them, but to be thankful for them.

The fact of human prayer to God and the prospect of divine response also argued against the Gnostic heresy that there is no direct contact between God and the human race. The apostle did not express his appreciation to any angelic intermediaries; rather, he utilized the blessed privilege of direct access to the presence of God (Heb. 4:14–16; 10:19–22).

The prepositional phrase, "for you," shows the scope of the prayer. The preposition (*peri*) conveys the concept of "around" (as in "perimeter"). The apostle literally prayed around the Colossians, encircling them with his requests. When a believer is surrounded by prayer, he is unlikely to succumb to the attacks of false moral and doctrinal teaching.

B. The Cause of Thanksgiving (1:4)

Thanksgiving is invariably prompted by the reception of a good report or gift. The cause for the apostolic thanksgiving is given in the participial phrase introduced by the words "since we heard" *(akousantes)*.[2] The plural indicates that both Paul and Timothy were dependent upon outside sources for their knowledge of the Colossian situation. The tense of the participle (aorist) reveals that they had heard all of the necessary data before they gave thanks. There is no inference that they were presently receiving new information. Undoubtedly they heard from Epaphras, who had traveled to Rome to give the apostle a firsthand report (1:7–8; 4:12). The Colossian ambassador revealed two reasons for thanksgiving.

1. Their faith

Two aspects of the Colossians' faith are stressed. *First,* it was specific and personal. The phrase literally reads, "the faith of you" *(tēn pistin humōn).* The usage of the definite article "the" *(tēn)* shows that Paul did not refer to the abstract principle of general faith, but that he complimented a particular action. The personal pronoun, "you," implies that the Colossians actively believed in the Lord.[3]

Second, that faith rested "in Christ Jesus." In the New Testament, three prepositions are used along with the verb "to believe" to manifest the scope of redemptive faith. A sinner puts his faith into *(eis)* Christ and causes it to remain in *(en)* Him; thus his faith rests upon *(epi)* the Savior. Mere faith cannot save anyone; it must have a valid object. Christ must always be the goal *(eis),* the sphere *(en),* and the foundation *(epi)* of spiritual faith. All three concepts embrace both the initial act of saving faith, which receives the righteousness of God and divine justification, and the continuance of faith, which produces the sanctified life. Men are justified by faith in Christ and they must walk by faith (Rom. 1:16–17; 5:1). Since faith comes only by hearing the proclaimed word of God, the Colossian believers must have been regenerated through the preaching of Epaphras or one of Paul's associates (Rom. 10:17).

[2] A causal usage of the aorist participle. Aorist verb forms refer to actions that occurred once in the past, and are completed.

[3] This is a subjective genitive, meaning that the word in the genitive case ("you") produced the verbal action of the noun preceding it ("faith").

2. *Their love*

Faith in God and love for God's children always go together. John wrote: "And this is his commandment, That we should believe on the name of his Son Jesus Christ, and love one another, as he gave us commandment" (I John 3:23). Note the order. Faith comes first, then love. Vertical faith precedes horizontal love, because love is the outworking of faith. Paul asserted that faith "worketh by love" (Gal. 5:6).

Two observations about the Colossians' love are set forth. *First,* it was divinely given. They possessed "the love" *(tēn agapēn),* that type which is an evidence of regeneration. Believers "are taught of God to love one another" (I Thess. 4:9). John commented: "We know that we have passed from death unto life, because we love the brethren" (I John 3:14). This love transcends mere human relationships (as seen in *philē* and *eros* types of love); rather, it reflects the nature of divine love *(agapē;* I John 4:8).

Second, this love reached out "to all the saints." The passage literally reads: "the love, the into all the saints one" *(tēn agapēn tēn eis pantas tous hagious).*[4] Although believers should love the entire world of lost men (John 3:16), the apostle commended these believers for their special love extended to all Christians, both those in their church and others throughout the Roman empire. They epitomized Christ's injunction:

> A new commandment I give unto you, That ye love one another; as I have loved you, that ye also love one another.
>
> By this shall all men know that ye are my disciples, if ye have love one to another (John 13:34–35).

Peter charged Christians to "love one another with a pure heart fervently" (I Peter 1:22). The adverb "fervently" *(ektenōs)* comes from the verb which Jesus used in His command to the man with the withered hand ("stretch forth"; Mark 3:5). A fervent love is a love which stretches out to others; it is not selfish or limited. This love is a fruit of the Spirit (I Cor. 13; Gal. 5:22).

---

[4]The italicized words "which ye have" were inserted to make a smooth English transition.

THE GIVING OF THANKS

II. FOR THE GOSPEL (1:5-6)

The word "for" serves as the transition to this new section. Actually, it is a preposition *(dia)* normally translated as "because of." The grammatical relationship of the prepositional phrase, "for the hope," to the preceding two verses is an enigma. Some scholars see hope as a third cause for thanksgiving, along with faith and love.[5] Others view hope as the reason behind the Colossians' faith and love, or as the motivation behind their love only. It is even possible to relate it to the main verb ("we give thanks") and to consider hope as the reason for Paul's gratitude. No grammarian can be dogmatic in this situation.

Regardless, the triad of faith, love, and hope often appears in Paul's epistles (I Cor. 13:13; I Thess. 1:3). It is impossible to have one without the others. What is significant is the omission of wisdom, the quality which the false teachers emphasized more than any other. Paul thanked God for the Colossians' faith, love, and hope, but not for their knowledge. Believers need to know that knowledge puffs up, but that love builds up (I Cor. 8:1).

A. The Gospel Brings Hope (1:5)

Paul asserted:

> For we are saved by hope: but hope that is seen is not hope: for what a man seeth, why doth he yet hope for?
> But if we hope for that we see not, then do we with patience wait for it (Rom. 8:24-25).

Hope has both an inward and an outward character; it is both subjective and objective.

1. This hope is in heaven

The objective reality of the future, rather than an eager anticipation, is stressed here. Four features of hope are enumerated. *First*, it is definite ("the hope"), as seen by the usage of the article. It is specific, not nebulous.

---

[5]If that were the case, the simple connective "and" would have been used to join the three words.

Second, hope is reserved. The verb construction, "laid up," stresses the security of that which has been set aside by God.[6] Peter rejoiced that believers had been born into a living hope by the resurrection of Christ "to an inheritance, incorruptible, and undefiled, and that fadeth not away, reserved in heaven for you" (I Peter 1:3–4). Christ promised that He would prepare a place for His own (John 14:1–3). In the parable of the pounds, the wicked servant confessed to the nobleman: "Lord, behold, here is thy pound, which I have kept laid up [same word] in a napkin" (Luke 19:20). The verb connotes preservation, without the possibility of loss.

Third, this hope is "for you" *(humin).* The media have often reported that some people have lived without any awareness of an inheritance bequeathed to them or that they were unable to gain access to a fortune because of legal or geographical barriers. The believer, however, knows he will receive all that God has promised.

Fourth, this hope is "in heaven." Literally, the phrase reads "in the heavens" *(en tois ouranois).* Every believer knows that he has been blessed "with all spiritual blessings in heavenly places in Christ" (Eph. 1:3). In heaven are his citizenship (Phil. 3:20), his city and country (Heb. 11:16; 13:14), his treasure (Matt. 6:20), and his Savior (Phil. 3:20). Although the hope involves things, it actually is centered in a person. Christ is "the blessed hope" (Titus 2:13).

This hope will find its realization when the believer receives his immortal, incorruptible body. This will occur when Christ returns to raise the dead and to change living believers (I Thess. 4:13–18), although Christians who die do enjoy some of the benefits of hope as they are in the heavenly presence of Christ.

2. This hope is in the gospel

The gospel message is that which joins the hope in the heart with the hope in heaven. The connective "whereof" is actually a

---

[6]*tēn apokeimenēn.* This is a present participle used with a perfect sense.

relative pronoun *(hēn)*, normally translated as "which." It definitely refers to the previously mentioned hope.[7]

Three observations can be made about this gospel. *First,* it must be proclaimed orally. The Colossians "heard before" *(proē-kousate);* thus, before Paul wrote and before the heretics invaded their church, the Colossians had heard the redemptive message and had responded in saving faith. What they heard was contained "in the word" *(en tōi logōi).* Sinners are not saved by studying the heavens or by watching the lives of Christians. They must hear the inscripturated word of divine grace. In the parable of the sower, Christ declared: "But he that received seed into the good ground is he that heareth the word, and understandeth it" (Matt. 13:23). With passionate concern, Paul questioned: "How then shall they call on him in whom they have not believed? and how shall they believe in him of whom they have not heard? and how shall they hear without a preacher?" (Rom. 10:14).

Second, the gospel involves "the truth." Christ is that truth (John 14:6). Both His divine-human person and His redemptive death and resurrection must be presented with biblical accuracy and logic. Men must be told in all honesty who they are, who He is, what He has done, and what they must do about it. Method and message must complement each other. With clear conscience, the apostle could say: "And my speech and my preaching was not with enticing words of man's wisdom, but in demonstration of the Spirit and of power" (I Cor. 2:4). It is always wrong to proclaim the truth in a wrong way or for a wrong reason (I Thess. 2:3–6). Paul defended the truth of the gospel against the Judaizers in Jerusalem and against the prejudiced Peter in Antioch (Gal. 2:5, 14). The Judaizers distorted the truth of justification by imposing circumcision as a requirement for salvation, and Peter violated the truth when he acted as if Jews were superior to Gentiles in the body of Christ.

Third, the gospel centers in Christ's redemptive death and resurrection (I Cor. 15:1–4). It literally means "a good message" *(euaggelion).* It brings good news to a guilty, condemned world of

---

[7]It is accusative feminine singular, agreeing in gender and number with its antecedent.

lost mankind in that it declares what God has graciously provided through Christ's death and resurrection.

B. The Gospel Bears Fruit (1:6)

The participial phrase, "which is come" *(tou parontos)*, refers to the gospel, not to the hope.[8] It literally translates "the one which is beside." The gospel came to the Colossians when it was originally preached to them, probably by Epaphras or by one of the apostle's associates. Three observations about its ability to bear fruit are given.

1. In all the world

Just before His ascension, Christ commanded the apostles to disciple "all nations" (Matt. 28:19), to go "into all the world" (Mark 16:15), and to witness of Him "unto the uttermost part of the earth" (Acts 1:8). During His earthly ministry, He restricted their preaching ministry to the Jews (Matt. 10:5–6). However, His rejection by Israel and His prediction of the forthcoming church age changed that earlier limitation.

Through His death, Christ provided reconciliation for the world (II Cor. 5:19); He was the propitiation for the sins of the whole world (I John 2:2). He died for all people: Jews and Gentiles, slaves and free, rich and poor, men and women. Paul did not mean that the gospel had gone out into the entire population of planet Earth, but that it had brought forth fruit wherever it had gone into the world. The universal application of the benefits of Christ's death thus refuted the exclusive claims of the Judaistic Gnostic teachers.

2. In you

The two areas of gospel fruitbearing ("in the world" and "in you") are both introduced by the connective "as" *(kathōs)*. Paul assured the Colossian believers that their conversion and their subsequent spiritual growth were the same as that produced by

---

[8]It is genitive neuter singular, in grammatical agreement with "the gospel."

the ministries of all the apostles throughout the Roman empire. They were not deficient, as the heretics suggested.

A harvest always has a beginning. The time of the initial fruit at Colosse is indicated by a clause which contains two key verbs: "since the day ye heard of it and knew the grace of God in truth." The believers "heard" *(ēkousate)* and understood fully *(epegnōte)* the gospel of grace. They knew that intellectualism and legalism were not the means of salvation. They comprehended the significance of Christ's death and resurrection. At the time of their conversion, they possessed a thorough and accurate saving knowledge *(epegnōte)* which surpassed that of the boastful Gnostics.[9]

3. Constantly

The verb "bringeth forth fruit" *(esti karpophoroumenon)*[10] stresses the fact that the gospel was still bearing fruit at the time Paul wrote, both in the world and at Colosse. People were continually being saved and growing in the faith. The middle voice of the participle shows that the gospel has innate ability to reproduce itself in the lives of its hearers. One person is saved after hearing the gospel, and then that person bears witness to another, who in turn becomes a Christian. The gospel also produces the fruit of the Spirit within the believer (Gal. 5:22–23). The gospel is like "the tree yielding fruit, whose seed was in itself, after his kind" (Gen. 1:12). It is like the earth which "bringeth forth fruit of herself; first the blade, then the ear, after that the full corn in the ear" (Mark 4:28).

III. FOR EPAPHRAS (1:7–8)

Epaphras of Colosse should not be confused with Epaphroditus of Philippi. Epaphras is mentioned only three times in the Scriptures (1:7; 4:12; Philem. 23), but enough is stated to show that he was an outstanding believer.

---

[9] The prepositional prefix *epi* intensifies the nature of this knowledge *(ginōskō)*. The title "Gnostic" is based upon this verb stem.

[10] It is a present middle participle in periphrastic construction with the present indicative of *eimi*.

STAND PERFECT IN WISDOM

A. His Titles

1. A servant

Paul identified Epaphras as "our dear fellowservant." The word "fellowservant" (sundoulou) literally reads "a joint slave." Since Christ had redeemed Paul and Epaphras, He owned both of them (I Cor. 6:19–20). Their wills were subject to His. This same title is later used of Tychicus (4:7).

The pronoun "our" shows that Paul linked Epaphras to himself and to Timothy. Although Paul was an apostle, he saw himself as a slave and equal to his associates.

Epaphras was "dear" in that he was "beloved" (agapētou): loved by God, the apostle, and the church.

2. A minister

Epaphras was also "a faithful minister of Christ." The word "minister" (diakonos) is the basis for the English term deacon. The Bible presents deacon-ministers in the official, technical sense as assistants to the pastor (Acts 6:1–7; I Tim. 3:8–13) and also in the general sense as those committed to service for others.

In the latter usage, angels ministered to Christ at His temptation (Matt. 4:11), and they also serve believers (Heb. 1:14). Women ministered by giving financial assistance to the apostolic group (Mark 15:40–41). Preparing dinner was a ministry (Matt. 8:15). Christ ministered by giving His life on the cross (Matt. 20:28). Phebe was a female servant, a deaconess of the church at Cenchrea (Rom. 16:1). Paul regarded himself and Apollos as ministers of the Word (I Cor. 3:5). The derivation of the word deacon is interesting. It is a compound word, based upon dia ("through") and konis ("dust"). The imagery suggests a person who quickly moves to perform his tasks and who creates a trail of dust by his haste.

Some manuscripts read "for us" rather than "for you." If "us" is the correct reading, then Epaphras was Paul's representative to Colosse. If "you" is the correct reading, then the church sent Epaphras as its emissary to minister to Paul in Rome. Epaphras was also a suitable servant in that he labored through intercessory prayer for the believers (4:12).

Epaphras was not an ordinary servant; rather he was "faithful" in the discharge of his duties. Faithfulness is the greatest qualification for Christian service (I Cor. 4:1–2).

B. His Deeds

1. The church learned from him

Epaphras probably both evangelized Colosse and edified the believers through his teaching. The verb "learned" *(emathete)* is the basis of the term *disciple*. Christ charged the apostles to "teach ["disciple"; *mathēteusate*] all nations" (Matt. 28:19), a process which involves evangelism, baptism, and instruction. Since Epaphras had taught the Colossians the basic doctrines of grace, his integrity was also under attack by the heretical philosophers.

2. He informed Paul

Paul also stated that Epaphras "declared unto us your love in the Spirit." The verb "declared" *(dēlōsas)* was used in the Greek papyri to indicate official, legal evidence. This means that Epaphras gave the apostle solid proof of the conversion of the Colossian believers, their subsequent spiritual growth, and their love for Paul. Paul then had no cause to question the validity of their confession. It was as real and genuine to him as to Epaphras.

Again, the presence of love is seen as an evidence of true spirituality (cf. 1:4). This was not mere human love developed to its fullest extent; this was a "love in the Spirit" *(agapēn en pneumati).*[11] The Holy Spirit had caused the Colossian believers to love God, each other, and the unseen apostle. Their attitude toward the Savior was reflected in their feelings toward Paul: "Whom having not seen, ye love" (I Peter 1:8). Paul was naturally thankful that he was included in their loving outreach (1:4).

Questions for Discussion

1. Do Christians adequately thank God for other believers?

---

[11]This is the only reference to the Holy Spirit in the book.

STAND PERFECT IN WISDOM

What often prevents the development of this gracious spirit? How can a Christian cultivate this attitude?

2. What kinds of faith are set forth in the Scriptures? What is the difference between a true and a false faith?

3. In what practical ways can saints manifest their love to others? to those they know? to unseen brothers?

4. What heavenly possessions await the believer? What is the difference between a genuine and a false hope?

5. In what ways has the gospel been robbed of its truth? How can error slip into evangelism? What effect does this have upon conversions?

6. Is lack of fruitbearing a sign of hypocrisy? of spiritual deadness? Can sterile hearts become fertile again?

7. What are the marks of genuine service for Christ? Do believers see themselves as slaves today?

3

The Worthy Walk
Colossians 1:9–13

Although the Christian life is a race to be run with purpose and patience (I Cor. 9:24–26; Heb. 12:1), it is normally described as a *walk*. Believers are charged not to walk after the flesh (Rom. 8:1), as men (I Cor. 3:3), in craftiness (II Cor. 4:2), by sight (II Cor. 5:7), according to the course of this world (Eph. 2:2), in the vanity of pagan mentality (Eph. 4:17), in a disorderly way (II Thess. 3:6), or in darkness (I John 1:6). Rather, they are exhorted to walk in newness of life (Rom. 6:4), after the Holy Spirit (Rom. 8:1, 4), honestly (Rom. 13:13), with brotherly love (Rom. 14:15), by faith (II Cor. 5:7), in the Spirit (Gal. 5:16), in good works (Eph. 2:10), as children of light (Eph. 5:8), circumspectly (Eph. 5:15), in wisdom (Col. 4:5), in the light (I John 1:7), and in truth (III John 3).

The above positive and negative characteristics describe the "worthy" *(axiōs)* walk of the believer. The apostle wrote to the Ephesians: "I therefore, the prisoner of the Lord, beseech you that ye walk worthy of the vocation [calling] wherewith ye are called" (Eph. 4:1). He charged the Thessalonians to "walk worthy of God" who had called them into his "kingdom and glory" (I Thess. 2:12). And he prayed that the Colossians "might walk worthy of the Lord unto all pleasing" (1:10). A worthy walk, therefore, is consistent with the divine purpose of redemption. It is lived in the will of God for daily experience. Its essence is to walk as Christ walked (I John 2:6).

STAND PERFECT IN WISDOM

I. FOUNDATION OF A WORTHY WALK (1:9)

Paul's prayer for the Colossians develops around two purpose clauses, both introduced by the connective "that" (1:9, 10). The second purpose actually is a result of the first. These are not coordinate clauses; rather, the first must be achieved in order for the second to occur.[1]

A. The Object of Human Prayer

Spirituality does not automatically happen. It involves willful interest and effort. Although a believer must work out his own salvation (Phil. 2:12), it is also true that he needs the assistance of others. He needs to be ministered unto as well as to minister. Here, Paul informs the Colossians that he is praying for their moral development, whereas later he asks for their prayers on his behalf (4:2–3).

1. Cause of the prayer

The opening words, "For this cause," reveal the reason behind the apostolic intercession. This definitely refers to the Colossians' love in the Spirit (1:8), but it also includes their faith in Christ, brotherly love, expectant hope, and fruitbearing (1:4–6). The plural, "we," is emphatic and points to both Paul and Timothy. The connective "also" (kai) means that the two joined with Epaphras in a ministry of prayerful concern. Of Epaphras, the apostle later commented: ". . . always labouring fervently for you in prayers, that ye may stand perfect and complete in all the will of God. For I bear him record, that he hath a great zeal for you" (4:12–13).

The time at which this prayer was initiated is indicated by the next phrase, "since the day we heard it." Paul and Timothy thus began their ministry of intercession when Epaphras reported to them about the spiritual vitality of the Colossian church.

---

[1]The first begins with *hina* followed by a subjunctive purpose clause, whereas the second is introduced by a purpose infinitive ("that ye might walk," *peripatē-sai*).

2. Nature of the prayer

Four observations can be made regarding the prayer. *First*, it was constant ("do not cease"). Paul and Timothy did not pray only once. They began their work of intercession, and then continued it. The present tense of the verb *(pauometha)* reinforces this conclusion.

Second, the prayer was intercessory ("for you," *huper humōn*). Although Paul was a prisoner in Rome, he was not concerned about himself. James charged believers to pray for each other (James 5:16). When they bear one another's burdens, they then practice the law of Christ (Gal. 6:2).

Third, the prayer was incorporated within Paul's devotion and worship ("to pray"). The word here used is the general word for prayer in the New Testament, always directed toward God and never to man *(proseuchomenoi)*.[2] The verb occurs eighty-five times and its noun *(proseuchē)* thirty-seven times. Genuine prayer is exercised under the control of the Holy Spirit (Rom. 8:15) and arises from a personal awareness of being one of God's own children (Rom. 3:26; Gal. 4:6).

Fourth, the prayer involved a specific request ("to desire"). This verb *(aitoumenoi)* originally meant "to want or to demand something as one's share," but this concept can never apply to the approach of a believing sinner to his Creator-God. However, God has asked His children to make requests of Him (Matt. 7:8). No Christian can demand that God do something, but he can ask Him for that which He has promised to give if he will make his request in the right way. The middle voice of the verb shows Paul's strong interest in seeing this petition granted. Unfortunately, too many saints offer perfunctory prayers for others. They are not emotionally interested, but they sense an obligation to mention names and needs. The apostle, however, involved himself emotionally when he prayed.

[2]The two English infinitives, "to pray" and "to desire," are actually Greek complementary participles tied to the main verb ("cease").

B. The Knowledge of His Will

The connective "that" *(hina)* introduces the content or initial purpose of the request.[3] It is not enough simply to pray for someone else. The petitioner must also ask God to accomplish specific goals in the life of that person. Three features of Paul's goals for the Colossians can be found in his request.

1. That the Colossians be filled by God

Believers can not fill themselves nor can they be filled by other saints. The passive voice of the verb ("might be filled," *plērō-thēte)* indicates that this ministry is performed by God through the Holy Spirit. Spiritual truth is imparted to spiritual hearts by the Spirit of God (I Cor. 2:10–12).

The verb means "to fill out to completion." It is frequently used of the fulfillment of Old Testament prophecies in New Testament events (Matt. 1:22; 2:15). Believers are instructed to be filled with joy and peace (Rom. 15:13), comfort (II Cor. 7:4), obedience (II Cor. 10:6), the fullness of God (Eph. 3:19), with the Spirit (Eph. 5:18), and the fruits of righteousness (Phil. 1:11). The adjective *(plērēs)* is used to refer to those who are full of faith and power (Acts 6:8), of the Holy Spirit (Acts 7:55), and of good works (Acts 9:36). In this book, the verb is used five times (1:9, 25; 2:10; 4:12, 17) and the noun twice (1:19; 2:9).

2. That the Colossians be filled with the knowledge of His will

The heretics emphasized knowledge *per se (gnōsis)*, but the word used in verse 9 stresses an intensive, thorough knowledge *(epignōsin)*.[4] The plan for the counteroffensive against the onslaught of false teaching was more knowledge, not ignorance nor an appeal to experience.

Paul refers to a specific knowledge, a perception of the divine mind ("of his will").[5] This deals with God's perceptive will for believers as expressed in the following verses (1:10–13). God will

---

[3]*Hina* may introduce grammatically a substantive clause ("that") or a purpose clause ("in order that").

[4]The prefix *epi* gives the idea of knowledge upon knowledge.

[5]Note the usage of the definite article before "knowledge."

always make known His will to His children who want to know and do it because they love it. A child of God must recognize the truth that the will of God offers the best avenue for his life even before he knows what that will is. The will of God is always manifested under the guidance of the Holy Spirit according to the proper interpretation of the Scriptures. God never directs His own to do that which is contrary to the revealed, inscripturated Word. To be filled with such knowledge, one must empty himself of his self-will (John 4:34; 6:38). With Christ, he must affirm: ". . . not my will, but thine, be done" (Luke 22:42).

3. That the Colossians be filled in wisdom and understanding

Paul prayed that the Colossian believers might be filled with the divine will "in all wisdom and spiritual understanding." The two adjectives, "all" and "spiritual," qualify both nouns; thus, the phrase means "all spiritual wisdom" and "all spiritual understanding." God's will pertains to all areas of the believer's life: vocational, marital, financial, and social. These areas are "spiritual" (*pneumatikēi*) in that the Holy Spirit who abides in every believer instructs the saint in the spiritual things of the Scriptures which He inspired (I Cor. 2:9–14). The unsaved man, devoid of the Holy Spirit, cannot perceive these things (I Cor. 2:14).

The two realms, wisdom and understanding, are distinctive, yet corollary.[6] The concept of "wisdom" (*sophia*) deals with what we should be and do, and the idea of "understanding" (*sunesis*) refers to how we accomplish those goals. The former possibly alludes to what we should believe, and the latter to how we should behave.

The word "wisdom" is found six times in the book (1:9, 28; 2:3, 23; 3:16; 4:5). Aristotle defined wisdom as "mental excellence in its highest and fullest sense." However, this pagan philosopher was aware of only "the wisdom of this world" (I Cor. 1:20). Wisdom includes general principles, the "whole range of mental faculties."[7]

---

[6]No definite article occurs with either noun and both serve as the objects of the single preposition: *en pasēi sophiāi kai sunesei pneumatikēi.*

[7]Homer A. Kent, Jr., *Treasures of Wisdom: Studies in Colossians and Philemon*, p. 40.

The term "understanding" occurs twice in the book (1:9; 2:2), and only five times elsewhere (Mark 12:33; Luke 2:47; I Cor. 1:19; Eph. 3:4; II Tim. 2:7). It is a compound word, meaning "to send" *(hiēmi)* and "with or together" *(sun)*.

Herbert M. Carson wrote that understanding is "the application of this basic wisdom to the various problems which present themselves to us and require a clear analysis before a decision can be taken."[8] It involves critical thinking about the complexities of life and a Spirit-guided solution which manifests biblical content. Such wisdom and understanding will always manifest genuine humility and a greater love and glorification of God.

II. MARKS OF A WORTHY WALK (1:10–13)

The second major purpose of the prayer is introduced by a Greek infinitive, "that ye might walk," *(peripatēsai)*. The divine will must be shown in a human walk. The walk pertains to life in its entirety, from regeneration to death.[9]

The goal of the worthy walk is the pleasure of God ("unto all pleasing"). This noun *(areskeian)* is found only here in the New Testament, although the verb form is used often. In classical Greek, this word referred to a "cringing and subservient habit, ready to do or say anything to please a patron."[10] By the first century, the word came to have both a good and a bad connotation. The bad connotation can be seen in Salome's dance to please Herod (Matt. 14:6) and in the false motivations of preachers (Gal. 1:10; I Thess. 2:4). The spiritual essence of the word, however, can be demonstrated in the desire of the Christian to please God in everything. This is not only the right thing to do, but it also brings fulfillment and personal satisfaction to the child of God. Believers please God when they complete their obligations to Him (I Cor. 7:32; I Thess. 2:4; 4:1; II Tim. 2:4), to family (I Cor.

---

[8]Herbert M. Carson, *The Epistles of Paul to the Colossians and to Philemon*, p. 35.

[9]*Peripatēsai* is a constative aorist infinitive.

[10]H. C. G. Moule, *Studies in Colossians and Philemon*, p. 72.

7:33–34), and to others (Rom. 15:2; I Cor. 10:33). In so doing, they follow the selfless example of Christ (Rom. 15:3).

The four marks of this pleasing, worthy walk are set forth in four participial phrases.

A. Fruitfulness (1:10)

1. The nature of bearing fruit

Bearing spiritual fruit is a human responsibility. The participle "being fruitful" is in the active voice (*karpophorountes*), whereas the verb form used of the gospel is in the middle voice (1:6). The gospel has innate fruitbearing properties, but the believer must actively yield himself to the indwelling Holy Spirit in order to produce fruit. Using the metaphor of the vine and the branches to show the relationship of Himself to the disciples, Jesus Christ said: "Abide in me, and I in you. As the branch cannot bear fruit of itself, except it abide in the vine; no more can ye, except ye abide in me" (John 15:4). The present tense of the participle shows that the child of God should constantly produce spiritual fruit, in contrast to the seasonal harvests of the natural creation.

The fruit is the life of Christ manifested in and through the believer (Gal. 2:20; Phil. 1:21). It is "fruit unto holiness" (Rom. 6:22). It begets a distinctive, spiritual temperament: "But the fruit of the Spirit is love, joy, peace, longsuffering, gentleness, goodness, faith, meekness, temperance" (Gal. 5:22–23). It is the evidence of genuine discipleship and results in the glorification of God (John 15:8).

2. The realm of bearing fruit

In their unsaved lives, Christians possessed fruit "in those things whereof [they] are now ashamed" (Rom. 6:21). The worthy walk, however, reveals fruit "in every good work." The believer should never make a distinction between the sacred and the secular. He must glorify God in everything that he does.

The "good work" (*ergōi agathōi*) is not the fruit; rather, the fruit must be produced in the sphere of every good work. A good work is that which corresponds to the goodness of God (Mark 10:18). This is a work that is innately good *(agathos)*, not that which appears to be beautiful to human observation *(kalos)*. Since no person can do such good, it can only be performed by God working through him (Rom. 3:12).

B. Knowledge of God (1:10)

1. It must increase

The participle "increasing" *(auxanomenoi)* denotes constant growth.[11] Homer A. Kent, Jr., observed that the verb form "depicts a fruit tree which yields its fruit and keeps on growing, in contrast to grain which produces its harvest and then dies."[12] The psalmist described this feature of the worthy walk in these words:

> Blessed is the man that walketh not in the counsel of the ungodly, nor standeth in the way of sinners, nor sitteth in the seat of the scornful.
> But his delight is in the law of the LORD; and in his law doth he meditate day and night.
> And he shall be like a tree planted by the rivers of water, that bringeth forth his fruit in his season; his leaf also shall not wither; and whatsoever he doeth shall prosper (Ps. 1:1–3).

The believer must continue to grow in grace (II Peter 3:18; same verb, *auxanete*). His capacity for God must grow larger.

2. It must be thorough

The goal of increase is literally "unto the full knowledge of God" *(eis tēn epignōsin tou theou)*.[13] To become a Christian, a sinner must have a saving knowledge. Christ explained: "And this is life eternal, that they might know thee the only true God, and Jesus Christ, whom thou hast sent" (John 17:3). Paul viewed his salvation experience as that moment when he first counted all

---

[11] Present middle participle.

[12] Kent, *Treasures of Wisdom*, p. 42.

[13] The critical text uses the instrumental of means or the locative of sphere *(tēi epignōsei)* rather than *eis* with the accusative case.

self-righteous achievements to be loss "for the excellency of the knowledge of Christ Jesus my Lord" (Phil. 3:8).

To become a spiritual Christian, however, one must have a seeking, sanctifying knowledge. The word "knowledge" *(epignō-sin)* implies an intense, personal, experiential awareness to which more can be added. The major motivation in the apostle's life was to know Christ (Phil. 3:10). Believers are commanded to grow in grace and in the knowledge of Christ (II Peter 3:18). This goal can be achieved only through a humble study of God's self-revelation through the Scriptures and in the application, under the control of the Holy Spirit, of biblical principles to the various facets of life.

To know God is to love Him; to love Him is to walk with Him and for Him in a worthy fashion.

C. Strength (1:11)

The third mark of the worthy walk is inner spiritual fortitude.

1. Source of strength

Strength is not gained in a once-for-all crisis experience; rather, it involves a lifelong process. The participle "strengthened" literally reads "being strengthened" *(dunamoumenoi)*.[14] The believer does not strengthen himself, but he must be submissive to God who provides the moral enablement. Elsewhere Paul commanded: "Be strong *[endunamousthe]* in the Lord, and in the power of his might" (Eph. 6:10).[15] The apostle also prayed that Christians might be "strengthened with might by his Spirit in the inner man" (Eph. 3:16).[16] With humble optimism, every saint should be able to confess: "I can do all things through Christ which strengtheneth *[endunamounti]* me" (Phil. 4:13). Both the indwelling Christ and Spirit are the source of this needed power. They minister through the Word of God (Ps. 119:28).

---

[14]Present passive participle.

[15]Present passive imperative, based upon the same verb as "strengthened."

[16]This verb for "strengthen" *(krataiōthēnai)* is different. It corresponds to the word "power" *(kratos)* in 1:11.

STAND PERFECT IN WISDOM

2. *Sphere of strength*

Believers are to be strengthened "with all might" *(en pasēi du-namei)*. The words "might" and "strengthened" come from the same Greek root; the phrase could be translated "strengthened in all strength" or "enabled in all enablement." The root word implies ability, power, and innate strength. The English word *dynamite* is based upon it. Christ taught that such inner ability resulted when the believer was filled by the Holy Spirit (Acts 1:8). The inclusive adjective "all" means that "for every requirement there is power available."[17] God never asks His children to do anything without first supplying them with the power to do it.

3. *Standard of strength*

God strengthens "according to his glorious power." The noun "power" *(kratos)* refers to supernatural strength. Of the twelve times it is used in the New Testament, eleven refer to God (Luke 1:51; Acts 19:20; Eph. 1:19; 6:10; Col. 1:11; I Tim. 6:16; I Peter 4:11; 5:11; Jude 25; Rev. 1:6; 5:13) and one refers to Satan (Heb. 2:14).

The phrase literally reads, "according to the power of His glory." The glory of God is the outward expression of who He is. At times it refers to the blinding brightness which radiates from His holy being, but it also expresses the demonstration of His attributes, such as power, grace, truth, mercy, and love (John 1:14; 2:11). God here reveals Himself through what He enables the believer to do with the ability which only He can provide.

4. *Goal of strength*

Weightlifters strengthen themselves to lift heavy weights, and football place-kickers "psych" themselves to kick the winning field goals. Believers too are enabled to produce unusual character traits. The preposition "unto" *(eis)* indicates that goal.

The goal is twofold: "unto all patience and longsuffering." The former term *(hupomonēn)* points to circumstances sent by God and the latter *(makrothumian)* to the endurance of things imposed by man.

[17]Carson, *Epistles of Paul*, p. 37.

The first virtue, "patience," is a compound word meaning "to remain under" *(menō and hupo)*. A person is patient when he remains steadfast under the difficult pressures of life. It is "not therefore so much a passive acceptance of the inevitable, as an active unrelenting endeavor even in spite of difficulty and trial."[18]

The second quality, "longsuffering," is literally "wrath that is put far away." One work of the sinful flesh is wrath (Gal. 5:20); the Spirit-controlled believer puts a distance between himself and this enemy. Long-suffering enables a Christian to tolerate people who try his patience (II Cor. 6:6). It permits him both to forgive and to forbear others in love (3:13). He does not have a quick temper.

The goal of this inner strengthening is humble endurance of trials "with joy." Patience and long-suffering without joy will lead to depression and a defeatist attitude. Joy gives optimism, triumph, and trust. The Christian must believe that God is working out His sovereign purpose through the situation (Rom. 8:28; James 1:2).

D. Thanksgiving (1:12–13)

A worthy walk is a thankful walk (cf. 1:3). The heretics charged that there is no direct contact between God and man, but the apostle claimed that the believer can give thanks personally and directly to his heavenly Father.

Three reasons are given to show why the Father is worthy of thanks. These reasons are indicated by the three main actions described in this passage. All three actions reveal God's intervention into the time-space universe to act directly in behalf of His own.

1. He made them meet (1:12b)

God "hath made us meet" in that He has qualified us to be spiritual heirs. The verb *(hikanōsanti)* looks back at conversion, when God enabled man to have a sufficient, acceptable position in Christ. The believer was not made deserving at that time, but he was placed into the Son who is deserving. Paul used the same

[18]Ibid.

word to demonstrate that his sufficiency *(hikanoi)* came from God, and not from himself (II Cor. 3:5).

The purpose of this divine qualification of believers was that they might "be partakers of the inheritance of the saints in light." The noun translated "partakers" *(merida)* is actually "part," referring to the portion, not to the person. Christians have been allocated a definite part of the eternal riches. They will share in the "many mansions" promised by Christ (John 14:2).

The Christians' part will be "of the inheritance of the saints." The Israelites looked upon Canaan as their inheritance, but the believer shares in the "inheritance incorruptible, and undefiled, and that fadeth not away, reserved in heaven" (I Peter 1:4). All regenerated sinners are God's "children, then heirs; heirs of God, and joint-heirs with Christ" (Rom. 8:17; cf. Gal. 4:7). They share equally in what Christ has provided through His redemptive death and resurrection. The term for "inheritance" *(klērou)* originally meant a pebble or a piece of wood used for the casting of lots (Acts 1:26), but later it came to refer to the allotted portion.

The Christian's portion is a holy inheritance. God the Father is light (I John 1:5), God the Son is light (John 1:9), and the holy city will be full of light (Rev. 21:23; 22:5). Concerning the unsaved Gentiles, Christ told Paul that He wanted "to open their eyes, and to turn them from darkness to light, and from the power of Satan unto God, that they may receive forgiveness of sins, and inheritance among them which are sanctified by faith that is in me" (Acts 26:18).

2. He delivered them (1:13a)

Two aspects of the deliverance are emphasized. *First*, it was a total, divine rescue. This verb form is used only of God in the New Testament (Matt. 6:13; 27:43; Luke 1:74; 11:4; Rom. 7:24; 15:31; II Cor. 1:10; Col. 1:13; I Thess. 1:10; II Thess. 3:2; II Tim. 3:11; 4:17–18; II Peter 2:7, 9). In fact, Christ is called "the Deliverer" (Rom. 11:26). The Triune God is involved in spiritual deliverance, but in this passage, the relative pronoun ("who") has as its antecedent the "Father." The aorist tense of the verb *(errusato)* reveals that the deliverance was decisively accomplished at the conversion of the sinner.

I. THE PROOF OF PREEMINENCE (1:14–18a)

Christ's exaltation is set forth in four basic relationships: to sin (1:14), to God (1:15a), to creation (1:15b–17), and to the church (1:18). He thus is preeminent because He is the redeemer, the revealer, the creator, and the head.

A. In Redemption (1:14)

1. Its sphere

The spiritual deliverance and transfer of the believing sinner have been made possible by Christ's redemptive death and resurrection. He is the personal sphere of salvation ("in whom"). Eternal life is not an abstract possession; rather, it is a mystical union with the living Savior. Christ came that men might have life, but He Himself is that life (John 10:10; 14:6). Paul wanted to be "found in him" (Phil. 3:9). Because a believer is in Christ, he enjoys "wisdom, and righteousness, and sanctification, and redemption" (I Cor. 1:30).

2. Its possession

The simple verb "we have" (echomen) indicates that redemption is a present possession. No doubt is indicated through any wishful expression such as, "We think that we have." Its enjoyment is not projected into the future: "We will have someday." Rather, this is a bold statement of fact.

3. Its meaning

All believers have literally "the redemption" (tēn apolutrōsin). The usage of the definite article shows that Paul referred to the one and only redemption accomplished by God through Christ (Rom. 3:24). The noun emphasizes the concept of release because of a paid ransom. It is used ten times in the New Testament in a compound form, which basically means "to set free from" (lutrōsis and apo). Freedom from the penalty and effects of sin in a spiritual emphasis (Luke 21:28; Rom. 3:24; 8:23; I Cor. 1:? 1:7, 14; 4:30; Col. 1:14; Heb. 9:15; 11:35). In cog? s, Christ gave His life "a ransom [lutron] for many" (

Second, the believers have been rescued "from the power of darkness" (ek tēs exousias tou skotous). This expression points to the kingdom of Satan, which is marked by sin and moral darkness (Eph. 6:12). The concept of darkness includes an opposition to the light as well as an absence of it. The unbeliever is not only without God in the world, but he is also against God. This is a realm of moral rebellion, insubordination, and creaturely independence. John wrote:

> And this is the condemnation, that light is come into the world, and men loved darkness rather than light, because their deeds were evil.
> For every one that doeth evil hateth the light, neither cometh to the light, lest his deeds should be reproved (John 3:19–20).

3. He translated them (1:13b)

The believing sinner has been "delivered from" and "translated into." The first action is negative, whereas the second is positive. The first must logically precede the second. An event from recent history illustrates this point. In 1980, there was an aborted attempt to deliver the American hostages from the besieged embassy in Teheran and to transfer them into the custody of the United States. By contrast, God has successfully delivered believers from "the power of darkness" and "translated [them] into the kingdom of his dear Son."

The verb "translated" (metestēsen) has been used of the geographical transfer of people from one country to another. In that sense, a believing sinner has been transported from darkness into light, from the kingdom of Satan into the kingdom of Christ, and from hell into heaven. The aorist tense of the verb again refers to the decisive transfer which occurred at the moment of conversion. Positionally, the believer already is in heaven (Eph. 2:6), but he must await the practical realization of that experience.

The phrase "his dear Son" is literally "the son of His love" (tou huiou tēs agapēs autou).[19] God the Father eternally loves God the Son (Matt. 3:17). This is a kingdom marked by love: love of

---

[19]Since "love" is a noun of action, the pronoun "his" is a subjective genitive.

God for the Son, love of the Son for the Father, love of both the
Father and the Son for the saints, love of Christians for God, and
love of believers for each other. This kingdom, ruled by the principle of love, must be contrasted with the satanic kingdom, domi-
nated by fear, slavery, and darkness.

Questions for Discussion

1. In what ways do believers try to determine the will of God
for their lives? Which ways are right? Which are wrong?

2. How does common sense relate to the disclosure of the divine will? Do they ever contradict each other? Why?

3. For what reasons do believers walk before the Lord today?
Give illustrations of the worthy walk for contemporary living.

4. Why do many believers lack spiritual fruit? Why do some
stop producing fruit?

5. How can we know God more fully? What are some of the
obstacles to this goal?

6. Why do believers lack joy in endurance? How can patience
and long-suffering be cultivated in each life?

7. Do believers praise the Son more than the Father for their
salvation? What is the proper biblical balance?

4

The Exaltation of Chri
Colossians 1:14–

The main error of the Judaistic Gnostic heresy centered i
concept of the person and redemptive work of Jesus C
Through their exaltation of angelic mediators between Go
man, the false teachers denied the real deity and humanity
incarnate Son of God (2:18–19). Through their emphasis o
ism and intellectualism, they denied the efficacy of Chris
stitutionary atonement and physical resurrection (2:13–1
reduced Christ to a creature, the most powerful and i
being within the universe, but nonetheless still a crea
was like God, but not the same as God.

In his refutation of this heresy, Paul has here given
key Christological passages in the New Testament
1:1–18; Phil. 2:5–11; Heb. 1:1–3). It contains positiv
rather than negative refutations. It clearly sets forth
deity of Jesus Christ, the physical reality of His inc
direct creation of the total universe, His death and
and His ontological relationship to the Father.

This detailed exposition about the Son actually d
the closing remarks of the apostle's prayer for
(1:9–13). With the mention of the "Son" (1:13)
series of three clauses, introduced by the re
"whom" and "who" (1:14, 15, 18). Within this fr
ther stressed the importance of the Son by the
the personal pronouns "he" and "him."[1]

[1]The personal pronoun *autos*, in various forms, is use
14–20.

20:28; Mark 10:45). He obtained "eternal redemption *[lutrōsis]*" for His people (Heb. 9:12). He "gave himself a ransom *[antilutron]* for all" (I Tim. 2:6). This last word stresses the substitutionary character of His atonement (*anti*, "in the stead of").

Other words are also used to depict the full picture of biblical redemption. All unregenerate men are viewed as slaves in the marketplace of sin, but Christ has bought *(agorazō)* them with the payment of His vicarious death. This purchase price, however, can be either rejected or received (I Cor. 6:19–20; II Peter 2:1). The provision was made for all, but its value is applied only to those who believe.

A second word *(exagorazō)* stresses the removal of the believing sinner out from the dominion of sin (Gal. 3:13; 4:4–5). This concept is used only of the saints.

4. Its means

Redemption is only "through his blood."[2] Men are not saved by Christ's birth, by His teaching, nor by His perfect example. In order to accomplish salvation, He had to die a predetermined type of death. Only death by crucifixion, with the shedding of blood, could produce the remission of sins (Heb. 9:22). The idea implied is physical death. The mere shedding of blood that was not part of the dying process had no efficacious value.

From the death of the innocent animal in the Garden of Eden to Christ's death on the cross, one can trace a continuity of bloody sacrifices. The redemption of Israel from bondage in Egypt occurred after the Passover lamb was killed and its blood was sprinkled over the doorways of believers' homes. In like manner, Christ, the antitype Passover lamb, had to die. The value of the lamb in the divine redemptive program was in its death, not in its life (John 1:29: I Cor. 5:7).

5. Its result

The practical result of redemption in the life of the believer is "the forgiveness of sins." Actually, this phrase is in apposition to

---

[2]The critical Greek text omits these words, but they are found in a parallel passage (Eph. 1:7).

"the redemption." The noun "forgiveness" *(aphesin)* comes from a verb, "to send" *(hiēmi),* and a preposition, "away from" *(apo).* Thus, the essence of forgiveness is the sending away of sins from a person who committed those sins. David rejoiced in this truth: "As far as the east is from the west, so far hath he removed our transgressions from us" (Ps. 103:12). The noun "forgiveness" occurs seventeen times in the New Testament, but only four times in the Epistles (Eph. 1:7; Col. 1:14; Heb. 9:22; 10:18). The verb *(aphiēmi),* however, is used often.

The word for "sins" in verse 14 *(hamartiōn)* has a more general meaning than any of its synonyms in the New Testament. It means "to miss the mark," as does an archer whose arrow falls short of the target. All unregenerate men have sinned in thought and deed and have fallen short of God's righteous character (Rom. 3:23). In a parallel passage, another word for sins is used *(paraptōmatōn;* Eph. 1:7). But whatever word is employed, men lost in sin are dead (Eph. 2:1).

B. In Revelation (1:15a)

Persons are not known as things are known. A person must choose to reveal himself before others can know him fully. If this is true of finite man, it is more true of the infinite God.

1. God is invisible

He literally is "the God the unseen one" *(tou theou tou aoratou).* The gods fabricated by the imaginations of sinful men are totally visible and creaturely. They have mouths, eyes, ears, noses, hands, and feet (Ps. 115:4–7). The psalmist concluded: "They that make them are like unto them" (Ps. 115:8). Paul commented that foolish men "changed the glory of the uncorruptible God into an image made like to corruptible man, and to birds, and fourfooted beasts, and creeping things" (Rom. 1:23).

The true and living God, however, is a spirit being (John 4:24). The essence of deity is spiritual, not material. The apostle wrote that God "only hath immortality, dwelling in the light which no man can approach unto; whom no man hath seen, nor can see" (I Tim. 6:16). John added: "No man hath seen God at any time"

(John 1:18). No man, who can be in only one place at one time, has ever viewed the infinite, eternal God, who can be everywhere at all times.

In the Old Testament period, men "saw" God who was invisible (Heb. 11:27). What they saw, however, were theophanies —appearances of God in visible form for the purpose of communication. When God Himself spoke to man, He used anthropomorphic expressions (such as *hand* and *eyes*) to describe His strength and sight. These divine manifestations were unique and temporary. God can never be limited by space and time. Even though the glory filled the temple as an indicator of divine presence, Solomon confessed that "the heaven and heaven of heavens" could not contain God (I Kings 8:27).

2. Christ is the image

Christ "is the image of the invisible God" in that He both represents and manifests God to the world. What is God like? Look at Christ, and you will see what God is like. The incarnate Son of God said to the disciples: ". . . he that hath seen me hath seen the Father" (John 14:9). Since there is an intrapersonal oneness and equality within the triune divine Being, the essence of the Father can also be seen in the Son. Christ has "declared" *(exēgēsato)* the Father (John 1:18). He has literally *exegeted* Him. He has led the essence of deity out into open view so that men could see God in action.

The word "image" *(eikōn)* was used of the head of a ruler minted upon a coin (Matt. 22:20). It was used to describe John's vision of the statue or idol of the Antichrist (Rev. 13:14). It also referred to the parental likeness in a child. In these illustrations, the image always pointed to that upon which it was based.

Adam was made in the image and likeness of God (Gen. 1:26). Man today is still "the image and glory of God" (I Cor. 11:7; cf. Gen. 9:6; Col. 3:10; James 3:9). Truth about God can be learned from an objective, biblical study of man. Since a man is a living personality, one can conclude that God also is personal, possessing intelligence, emotions, and a will to choose. Since man has an innate sense of oughtness (a conscience) in his spiritual self, God also must be a moral, spirit being. Man, however, is like God, but he is not the same as God. He *was made* in the image of God.

On the other hand, Christ *is (estin)* the image of God (II Cor. 4:4). He did not become the image of God at His incarnation; rather, He is the eternal image of the eternal, invisible Father. As the Son of the Father (1:12–13), He is the "exact reproduction."[3] Man is a finite image, but Christ is the perfect, infinite image. This eternal relationship became visible through the incarnation and the subsequent manifestation in Christ's life, miracles, and words. As the perfect representative, only He could say: "He that honoureth not the Son honoureth not the Father which hath sent him" (John 5:23). Only God could reveal God.

C. In Creation (1:15b–17)

The next area of Christ's preeminence pertains to the created world. Since the false teachers stressed an angelic cosmogony, it was essential for Paul to set forth the proper doctrine of creation. Christ is set forth as the direct Creator-God in two ways: His title and His work.

1. His title (1:15b)

Christ is "the firstborn of every creature" *(prōtotokos pasēs ktiseōs).* The title connotes both priority and sovereignty. He existed before the world was created and He is the ruler over that creation. The fact of His voluntary subordination to the Father and subsequent incarnation did not abrogate this innate authority. At this moment He still *is* the first-born of every creature.

Some people have suggested that this phrase really teaches that Christ Himself was a creature, the first created by God and through whom God created all other things.[4] This heresy, however, is contradicted by the context. The passage does not say that He *became* a creature or that He was the first creature to be

---

[3]Everett F. Harrison, *Colossians: Christ All-sufficient*, p. 32.

[4]This is the theological position of the Jehovah's Witnesses, a group which denies both the Trinity and the deity of Christ.

made. If that had been the intent of the apostle, he could have used a different word: "first-created" *(prōtoktistos)*. Rather, Paul asserted that Christ created and that He existed before creation (1:16–17). If He were a "thing," how could He exist before He came into existence?

In its basic meaning, *prōtotokos* meant "the first one born" in a family. In Near Eastern culture, the eldest son, by right of being born first, received the birthright which entitled him to a double inheritance and family leadership upon the death of the father. The idea of supremacy soon overshadowed the concept of temporal priority. God thus established Israel as His "firstborn," the sovereign nation, even though many other nations existed before Israel (Exod. 4:22). God has planned to elevate the Son of David, the Messiah, as His "firstborn, higher than the kings of the earth" (Ps. 89:27). Jesus Christ, as the physical first-born of Mary and the legal first-born of Joseph, is that promised sovereign (Matt. 1:25; Luke 2:7).

Because He is who He is, one day every created being will bow before Him and acknowledge His sovereign deity (Phil. 2:10–11).

2. His work (1:16–17)

Christ's preeminence as the creator is now indicated in five key statements.[5] The first three center in three prepositional phrases: "by [in] him," "by him," and "for him." The fourth sets forth His uncreated preexistence ("before all things") and the fifth presents the ministry of preservation ("by him all things consist").

First, He is the *sphere* or *domain* of creation. The phrase "by him" literally reads "in him" *(en autōi)*. The Gnostic heretics taught that creation centered in a series of angelic beings, whereas the apostle affirmed that it centered in one person. Both the plan to create and the power to create resided in Him. He was the originator, both the architect and the builder. Creation was within His domain.

The object of creation was "all things" *(ta panta)*. This concept

---

[5]The verse begins with "for" or "because" *(hoti)*. Here are the proofs for His rulership over creation.

embraces the totality of the created universe, in both time and space. All things, collectively and individually, came from Him. From within His will and might proceeded the complex universe, although He must not be identified with it. He still remains both transcendent and immanent. The presence of the created world did not diminish His power or omnipresence.

The scope of the creation is then made specific in three areas. First, it reaches every locality—"that are in heaven, and that are in earth." The former includes the stars, the planets, and all other astronomical phenomena, whereas the latter points to both living and inanimate objects on planet Earth. Second, it envelops all kinds—"visible and invisible." The false teachers espoused the principle of dualism: material things are innately evil and immaterial things are intrinsically good. They denied that God directly created the physical world. But the two worlds—seen and unseen by the senses, natural and supernatural—were both created by Christ. Third, it incorporates all ranks—"whether they be thrones, or dominions, or principalities, or powers." These four classifications are used elsewhere to describe the world of angels, both holy and evil spirit beings (2:10; Eph. 1:21; 3:10). They are not in any descending order of importance, because a partial reverse order is given elsewhere (Eph. 6:12). In the Gnostic series of angelic emanations, a superior being created an inferior creature, and the latter in turn produced yet another lesser one. Christ, however, created all spirit beings instantaneously, directly, and out of nothing.

Second, Christ is the *agent* or *means* of creation. The phrase "by him" is literally "through him" *(di' autou)*. The three persons of the Triune God all actively participated in the work of creation: "In the beginning God *[Elohim]* created the heaven and the earth" (Gen. 1:1). The term *Elohim* refers to the trinitarian oneness. If a distinction of work assignment can be discovered, then the Father was the source of creation, the Son its agent, and the Spirit its preserver (Gen. 1:3; I Cor. 8:6). The same preposition *(dia)* is elsewhere used of Christ's creative agency: "All things were made by him: and without him was not anything made that was made" (John 1:3). The Father made the ages of time through the Son (Heb. 1:2).

Third, Christ is the *purpose* or *goal* of creation. All things are "for him," or literally "unto him" *(eis auton)*. Creation has meaning only when it points to Christ. Men should praise Him when they view the minute complexities of life through a microscope or the vastness of the universe through a telescope. Glory should be attributed to Him, not to a series of angelic emanations, to an impersonal Mother Nature, or to an atheistic principle of evolution.

The change in tenses of the two verbs for creation should be noted. The first *(ektisthē)* looks back to the creative act when everything came into being out of nothing through the expression of God's divine will. The second *(ektistai)* views creation as it presently stands. The contemporary universe is not the result of an ongoing creation process; rather, it is the permanent result of a past creative act.[6]

Fourth, Christ is *prior* to all creation. Verse 17 places great emphasis upon His person: "And he [himself, *autos*] is before all things."[7] The verb "is" *(esti)* indicates His eternal existence, an attribute of deity. Mere preexistence could have been set forth with the verb "was." However, the text states that He *is* before all things, not that He *was* before all things. This verb structure can refer only to God. On earth Jesus claimed to be the timeless Jehovah who spoke to Moses: "Verily, verily, I say unto you, Before Abraham was, I am" (John 8:58; cf. Exod. 3:14). He was with the Father "before the world was" (John 17:5). He eternally is in the form of God, sharing equally the essence of deity (Phil. 2:6).

Fifth, Christ is the *preserver* or *sustainer* of creation. He is the sphere in whom both creation and preservation operate. The phrase "by him" actually reads "in him" *(en autōi)*. The verb "consist" *(sunestēke)* means "to stand together, to hold together, or to cohere." His work of creation finds permanency in His work of preservation which began during the creation week and continues into the present.[8] He rested on the seventh day from His creative activity, but He did not cease His direct control of the universe

---

[6]The first verb is in the aorist tense and the second is in the perfect.

[7]The personal pronoun *autos* has intensive use here and also appears at the beginning of the sentence.

[8]The verb is perfect active indicative.

(Gen. 2:1–3; John 5:17). He always is "upholding all things by the word of his power" (Heb. 1:3). It is "by the word of God" that the world stands, and it is only by that same word that the universe will one day perish (II Peter 3:5).

D. In Headship (1:18)

H. C. G. Moule astutely observed that "the Head of Nature is the Head of Grace."[9] The focus on Christ's preeminence now changes from the old natural creation to the new spiritual creation. The creator now becomes the redeemer. Personal salvation was mentioned earlier (1:14), but that emphasis was upon what man obtained. In verse 18, the stress is upon what Christ gained through His death and resurrection. Three titles are given to describe this exalted position.

1. He is the head

Paul wrote: "And he is the head of the body, the church." The personal pronoun *(autos)* is again very emphatic and intensive here: "He Himself is the head." Only He qualifies to be recognized as this spiritual leader.

The two terms "body" *(sōmatos)* and "church" *(ekklēsias)* are in apposition to each other and describe the same entity. Since the definite article ("the") is used before each of them, the terms indicate a limited, specific group. But what is the body or the church?

The rise of the church was first predicted by Christ after His rejection by Israel became apparent: "I will build my church; and the gates of hell shall not prevail against it" (Matt. 16:18). He then informed His disciples that He would have to be killed and be resurrected in order to lay the foundation for the church (Matt. 16:21).[10] After His ascension into heaven, the Father officially established Christ as the head of the body, the church (Eph. 1:20–23). From this exalted position, Christ sent the Holy

[9]H. C. G. Moule, *Studies in Colossians and Philemon*, p. 81.
[10]The word "church" occurs only twice in the Gospels (Matt. 16:18; 18:17). The Greek term *(ekklēsia)* means "a called-out group."

66

Spirit into the world as He had promised and prayed (John 14:16; 15:26; Acts 1:5). It is by the baptism in the Holy Spirit that believing sinners are united with each other and with Christ to form the one true church (I Cor. 12:12–13; Eph. 4:4–6). The body of Christ (the church) therefore constitutes the entire group of saved people from the day of Pentecost (Acts 2:1–4) to the time of Christ's return to take His people into His presence (I Thess. 4:13–18).

As "the head" (*hē kephalē*) of the church, Christ has functional authority over His people. The church forms *His* body, *His* church, and *His* sheep (John 21:17).[11] The word "head" often refers to the head of the natural body (Matt. 6:17). It is also used metaphorically of the headship of the husband over the wife, of Christ over man, and of God over Christ (I Cor. 11:3–5; Eph. 5:23). When Israel rejected Christ through the crucifixion, that event actually caused Him to become the head of the corner for the church (Matt. 21:42; Acts 4:11; Eph. 2:20; I Peter 2:7). The church thus draws its sustenance and direction from Him (Eph. 4:15–16).

Unfortunately, the Colossian heretics denied to Christ His rightful position. They did not properly esteem the head when they wrongfully elevated the role of angels (2:18–19).

2. He is the beginning

The term "beginning" (*archē*) is a singular form, related to a plural word translated earlier as "principalities" (*archai;* 1:16). It has multiple usage because its word stem (*arch*) is the basis of two concepts: "to rule" (*archō*) and "to begin" (*archomai*). It often refers to the start of something (Matt. 19:4; Mark 1:1), but it can also point to political power (Luke 12:11; 20:20) and to supernatural rule (Rom. 8:38; Eph. 3:10).

This title for Christ is found only here and in the Book of Revelation.[12] In that closing canonical book, He is depicted as "the be-

---

[11]That it is called the church of Christ or the church of God (Matt. 16:18; John 21:17; Acts 20:28; I Peter 5:2) serves as a proof that Christ is God.

[12]The term *archē* is contained in a compound form *archēgos,* translated as "Prince" (Acts 3:15; 5:31), "captain" (Heb. 2:10), and "author" (Heb. 12:2).

ginning and the ending" (Rev. 1:8; 21:6; 22:13) and as "the beginning of the creation of God" (Rev. 3:14). Using this latter phrase, some people have argued that Christ was the first creature to be created by God; however, if that thesis were true, how could He be both the beginning and the ending, the first and the last creature to be made?

Christ is "the beginning" in that He originated both the natural and the spiritual creations. He created the worlds and He redeemed the church; thus only He qualifies to be the ruling head in both areas. In fact, He is "the head of all principality and power" (2:10).

3. He is the first-born

Christ is "the firstborn from the dead" (*prōtotokos ek tōn nekrōn*). He is the sovereign ruler of nature in that He brought life out of nothing (1:15) and He is the authoritative head of the church in that He brought life out of death. Only Christ can say: "I am he that liveth, and was dead; and, behold, I am alive for evermore, Amen; and have the keys of hell and of death" (Rev. 1:18).

During His earthly ministry, Christ raised at least three people out of physical death: the daughter of Jairus (Matt. 9:18–26), the widow's son at Nain (Luke 7:11–18), and Lazarus (John 11:38–44). Through delegated authority, the apostles also raised the dead in their first preaching journey (Matt. 10:8). These resurrections, however, were restorations to normal physical life. All of these people later died again. On the other hand, Christ was the first to come out of death in an immortal, incorruptible body.

This event established Christ in His rightful position as the supreme ruler of the realm of the dead. Through His death and resurrection, Christ destroyed Satan who heretofore had the power to keep men in the realm of death (Heb. 2:14).

The term "the dead" (*tōn nekrōn*) literally means "the dead ones." It refers to people, not to a place or to the principle of death. At His death, Christ went into paradise, the place of comfort within Sheol or Hades, which is the realm of departed human spirits (Luke 16:19–31; 23:43; Acts 2:25–31). When He arose, Christ left that realm and united Himself to a resurrected body.

He alone has the authority over death and hell (Rev. 1:18).

As the first-born, Christ will call all men out of death to stand in judgment before Him (John 5:28–29). He then has the authority both to permit believers to spend eternity in the holy city and to consign the unsaved to everlasting torment in the lake of fire.

II. THE DECLARATION OF PREEMINENCE (1:18b)

The connective "that" *(hina)* shows the purpose for the works of creation and redemption.

A. The Gaining of Preeminence

As God, before and after creation, Christ possessed an innate sovereignty. By His incarnation, death, resurrection, and ascension, He obtained a new type of preeminence. He had the former as God, but He gained the latter as the God-man.

The verb "might have" *(genētai)* literally means "might become." It was used of things coming to exist out of nothing and of the incarnation (John 1:3, 14). Thus, Christ became after His resurrection what He was not before His incarnation.

Again, the personal pronoun "he" *(autos)* is very emphatic. Only He qualifies for this preeminence, and it extends to "all things."

B. The Meaning of Preeminence

This is the only place in the New Testament where the word "preeminence" *(prōteuōn)* occurs. The Greek word is found in a compound form *(philoprōteuōn)* of an arrogant church leader, Diotrephes, "who loveth to have the preeminence among them" (III John 9).

The word is actually a participle meaning "to have first place." Coupled with the main verb, it denotes a permanent position of priority and authority. As the Creator-Redeemer who has both a divine nature and a human nature united within His single person, Christ has become preeminent over the realms of men and angels, both good and evil, throughout eternity (Phil. 2:9–11).

STAND PERFECT IN WISDOM

Questions for Discussion

1. How shallow is the believer's comprehension of the concept of biblical redemption? Is there a scarcity of doctrinal preaching today?

2. How can human forgiveness express divine forgiveness? What are the similarities? differences?

3. How can the doctrines about the Trinity and the deity of Christ be successfully presented to evangelical churches? How can those concepts be defended against attacks? What groups do not accept these two basic doctrines today?

4. Can Christ receive any glory if believers accept the idea of theistic evolution? In what ways are evolution and biblical creationism contradictory?

5. How can we distinguish between God's ordinary activity in the preservation of the universe and His extraordinary activity through miracles?

6. What is the difference between the universal church and the local church? How can the headship of Christ be applied to the operations of the local church? of a family?

7. In what practical ways can Christ be given the preeminence in all things within the life of each Christian?

5

The Work of God and Man
Colossians 1:19–29

In the ministry, men are "labourers together with God" (I Cor. 3:9). Man needs the power of God, and God works through the instrumentality of man. In an outreach to the world, the Holy Spirit and the believer must witness together as a team (John 15:26–27). The Christian must live a godly life and must speak words of truth, whereas the Spirit must convict the unregenerate hearts of sin, righteousness, and judgment (John 16:7–11).

In this section of the book, Paul stresses both human effort and divine enablement in the works of evangelism and discipleship (1:29). The apostle is the minister who preaches (1:23, 25, 28), but God reconciles and makes known (1:21, 27). Both God and Paul want to present each believer perfect before Christ (1:22, 28).

I. THE PLEASURE OF THE FATHER (1:19–23a)

The causal connective "for" (hoti) shows that the basis for the preeminence of the Son was the pleasure of the Father. In the Greek text, no grammatical subject is expressed.[1] Three possible subjects have been suggested: Christ, all the fullness,[2] and the Father. First, it is both theologically and grammatically unlikely that Christ would be both the sphere ("in him") and the subject of the verb, and that He would be both the reconciler and the

[1]Note that the words "the Father" are in italics.
[2]Translation in the RSV.

means of reconciliation (1:20–21). *Second,* to make the fullness the subject, the concept has to be personified. Also, it would equate the fullness with the one who reconciles (1:20).[3]

The *third* and best view is that the Father "pleased" *(eudokēse)* that these things happen. The verb is used of the pleasure or decision of unregenerate men (II Thess. 2:12), of believers (Rom. 15:26; II Cor. 12:10), and of God. It is never used of Satan, evil angels, or holy angels. Whenever God is the subject, it specifically refers to the Father (Matt. 3:17; Luke 12:32; Gal. 1:15; Eph. 1:5). In such instances, His pleasure is synonymous with His will or predetermined plan.

A. For Christ (1:19–20)

The Father's plan involved two aspects for the Son. The first pertained to fullness "in him" *(en autōi,* 1:19) and the second to reconciliation "by him" *(di' autou,* 1:20). The former refers to His incarnate person, whereas the latter points to His redemptive work.

1. Fullness (1:19)

Three truths concerning the Son are enumerated here. *First,* the fullness of God dwells "in him." It was not *around, upon,* or *under* Him; rather, it was *in* Him.[4] No creature, man or angel, could qualify as the tabernacle for the divine fullness.

Second, the infinitive "dwell" *(katoikēsai,* "to take up residence") points to the event of the incarnation.[5] Just as Mary and Joseph came to live in Nazareth (Matt. 2:23), so God the Son in His total deity came to dwell within a human body (2:9). As God, the Son possessed the complete fullness of the divine essence by eternal, innate right. The Father did not please that the Son should become deity before the incarnation or at the incarnation;

---

[3]Two infinitives, "to dwell" and "to reconcile," develop out of the main verb "pleased." The word "fullness" is in the neuter gender, whereas the participle, "having made peace," is in the masculine.

[4]This prepositional phrase is especially emphatic, occuring immediately after the connective "for" in the Greek text.

[5]Aorist active infinitive.

the Son was, is, and forever shall be God, equal to the Father within the ontological Trinity. In the plan of God, which involved the subordination of the Son in order to provide redemption, there was no diminishing of the divine attributes when God the Son took to Himself a perfect and complete humanity. God cannot be less than what He is, and the Son's total submission to and dependence on the Father did not change that unalterable truth. Second-century Corinthian Gnosticism taught that the spirit of the divine Christ came upon the man Jesus at baptism and left at the crucifixion. That heresy denied the hypostatic union—the fact that Christ possessed two natures, divine and human, within His single person.

Third, the phrase "all fulness" *(pan to plērōma)* refers to the total essence of deity. In classical Gnosticism, the concept referred to the total number of aeons or emanations which formed the bridge between God and man. As the eternal Son, Christ had all of the divine fullness, and when He became man, He manifested that essential fullness in official, redemptive acts. On earth, believers saw "his glory, the glory as of the only begotten of the Father, full of grace and truth" (John 1:14). All believers have enjoyed the benefits of His fullness redemptively expressed: "And of his fulness have all we received, and grace for grace" (John 1:16).

2. Reconciliation (1:20)

Five aspects of reconciliation are set forth. *First*, the *meaning* of "to reconcile" *(apokatallaxai)* is "to change completely."[6] Before the entrance of sin, God and man experienced unbroken friendship; when man sinned, that communion was interrupted. Man turned away from God. In reconciliation, the barriers are removed so that man can return to God. It is never said in Scripture that God is reconciled or that both God and man are reconciled.[7] Reconciliation is manward only (II Cor. 5:18–20). It is provisional in that man must willfully accept its condition of re-

---

[6]Note the intensive usage by the double prefix of two prepositions, *apo* and *kata*.

[7]In the reconciliation of two opposing human parties, a different Greek verb is used *(diallassō;* Matt. 5:24).

pentant faith. It renders men savable, but it does not force salvation upon them.

Second, the *means* is by Christ. The prepositional phrase "by him" *(di' autou)* is used twice in the verse to emphasize that point.

Third, the *goal* is "unto himself" *(eis auton)*. God chose to bring all men back to Himself for His glory. He is "not willing that any should perish, but that all should come to repentance" (II Peter 3:9).

Fourth, the *basis* of reconciliation is the cross ("having made peace through the blood of his cross"). Man rebelled and has waged war against God ever since. Elsewhere, Paul wrote: "For he [Christ] is our peace, who hath made both one, and hath broken down the middle wall of partition between us" (Eph. 2:14). Man erected the barrier and Christ knocked it down. This peace extends to all saved men, both Jews and Gentiles (Eph. 2:17). This provision of peace through reconciliation was made when men were "enemies" (Rom. 5:10).

This spiritual peace was gained "through the blood of his cross." He had to die; He had to die as a sacrifice; and He had to die on a cross. Blood had to be shed (Lev. 17:11; Heb. 9:22) in a prescribed way at a definite place (Gal. 3:13). The value of the death, however, is inseparably connected to the intrinsic worth of the dying person. It was the blood of the Creator-Redeemer in whom the fullness of God dwelt.

Fifth, the *object* of reconciliation was the universe ("all things"; 1:20). It incorporates the scope of the created world ("whether they be things in earth, or things in heaven"; cf. 1:16). The universe became unclean through angelic and human sin (Job 15:15; 25:5). The world of plants and animals suffered damage because of the sin of man (Gen. 3:17–18; Rom. 8:19–22). Christ died to purify both heaven and earth (Heb. 9:23). The benefits of His death will be manifested to this total domain in the millennium and throughout the eternal state.

B. For Believers (1:21–23a)

There is a change now from the general to the particular, from the provision of reconciliation to its actualization, and from "all things" to "you." As representative of all the redeemed, the Colossian believers are reminded by the apostle to contemplate the spiritual work of God in its triple perspective: past, present, and future.

1. Their past (1:21–22a)

A contrast is made between the Colossians' pagan past ("sometime," *pote*) and Christian past ("yet now," *nuni de*). The former refers to their lost spiritual position or standing, whereas the latter refers to the time when they were saved and entered into a position of acceptance before God.

Five concepts describe the Colossians' unregenerate condition. *First,* they all equally were under the penalty and power of sin (Rom. 3:9). The second person plural pronoun "you" *(humas)* included all of the Colossian believers, both corporately and individually, both Jew and Gentile. In their practice of sin, they undoubtedly differed, but not in their position. They were all totally depraved.

Second, they "were alienated." Their alienation continued from their conception to their conversion, and manifested their position of spiritual estrangement in Adam (Rom. 5:12–21).[8] Alienation means "to be a foreigner, a stranger, and to have what belongs to another" *(allotrios)*. The verb *(apallotrioō)* appears only three times in the New Testament. The unsaved are "aliens from the commonwealth of Israel" (Eph. 2:12) and "alienated from the life of God through the ignorance that is in them, because of the blindness of their heart" (Eph. 4:18).

Third, the Colossians were "enemies" *(echthrous)*. It is one thing to be estranged from someone; it is another thing to act in a hostile manner toward that one. The Colossians actively opposed God and willfully broke His moral law. Christ told the disciples to love their enemies, and Christ demonstrated that charge by dying for His enemies (Matt. 5:44; Rom. 5:10).

Fourth, the Colossians had mental enmity ("in your mind").

---

[8]This is a perfect passive participle in periphrastic construction: *ontas apēllotri-ōmenous*.

This word *(dianoiai)* concentrates on the thoughts and decisions within man. Intelligence is part of the image of God in man and is therefore good. God thinks, and so do men. Men were created to think God's thoughts after Him. The unsaved, however, do not "like to retain God in their knowledge" (Rom 1:28). Their thinking is both humanistic and antisupernaturalistic because their minds have been blinded by the ultimate enemy, Satan (Matt. 13:19, 28; II Cor. 4:4). Their carnal mind is at enmity with God, "for it is not subject to the law of God, neither indeed can be" (Rom. 8:7).

Fifth, the mental enmity manifests itself "by wicked works." Thoughts and actions go together. With a reprobate mind, people "do those things which are not convenient" (Rom. 1:28). They are candidly "haters of God" (Rom. 1:30).

In spite of these negative traits, God "reconciled" these Colossians. The aorist tense looks back to the time when they were saved by faith in Christ who had made provision for their reconciliation at the cross. The propitiatory sacrifice took place "in the body of his flesh through death." The heresy claimed that material entities are innately evil and that immaterial concepts are intrinsically good. That false dichotomy is negated by the fact that Christ provided salvation in a physical body of skin, bone, and blood, and that human sin originated in thought processes. Christ "abolished in his flesh the enmity" (Eph. 2:15). The means of reconciliation is literally "through the death" *(dia tou thanatou)*. The definite article ("the") points to a particular type of death, namely, the cross. He "became obedient unto death, even the death of the cross" (Phil. 2:8).

2. Their future (1:22b)

The *purpose* behind the pleasure of the Father and the reconciliation of the Son is "to present" saved sinners in heaven for all eternity. The verb *(parastēsai)* means "to stand beside." In that future day, believers will stand beside each other totally dressed in the righteousness of Christ, before almighty God ("in his sight"). The aorist tense points to that time when the entire body of Christ, the true church, will be presented. This will occur at the return of Christ when resurrected Christians and living believers will be caught up into heaven to meet the Savior (I Thess. 4:13–18). Paul gave this practical application of that great event:

> Husbands, love your wives, even as Christ also loved the church, and gave himself for it;
> That he might sanctify and cleanse it with the washing of water by the word,
> That he might present it to himself a glorious church, not having spot, or wrinkle, or any such thing; but that it should be holy and without blemish (Eph. 5:25–27).

The *manner* of presentation involves three aspects. *First,* all believers will be presented as "holy" *(hagious)*. This will be the climax of the divine work of sanctification.[9] All redeemed are positionally set apart in Christ today; thus they are saints, or holy, now. They are also striving to be holy in their daily experiences, but at the return of Christ, they will be forever set apart from the effects of sin. When used together with the adjective "unblameable," the word "holy" stresses the possession of imputed righteousness.

Second, all believers will be "unblameable" *(amōmous)*, without spot or blemish. Elsewhere, Paul wrote that God "hath chosen us in him before the foundation of the world, that we should be holy and without blame [same word] before him in love" (Eph. 1:4). Blamelessness is the opposite of imputation in that it denotes the total removal of sin and guilt from the believing sinner.

Third, all believers will be "unreproveable" *(anegklētous)*. This compound word literally means "not to be called in." It is a legal term. No charge of condemnation nor sentence of eternal death can ever be brought against believers in the court of divine justice. Compare Paul's rhetorical question: "Who shall lay any thing to the charge [same word stem] of God's elect? It is God that justifieth. Who is he that condemneth? It is Christ that died . . ." (Rom. 8:33–34).

These three truths are the possession of each Christian today, and God's faithfulness guarantees that the acceptable standing will endure until the day of Christ (I Cor. 1:8).

[9]See exposition under "saints" (1:2), p. 25.

3. Their present (1:23a)

Doctrinal integrity is a sign of genuine reconciliation. Continuance in the faith is a necessary prerequisite to presentation in heaven. John wrote: "Whosoever transgresseth, and abideth not in the doctrine of Christ, hath not God. He that abideth in the doctrine of Christ, he hath both the Father and the Son" (II John 9).

The conditional particle ("if") seems to imply that a person can lose his salvation (reconciliation and presentation) if he fails to "continue in the faith." The apostle, however, taught just the opposite. He assumed that the Colossians were continuing in the faith. This conditional clause can be translated: "If indeed ye continue in the faith, and I believe that you are doing so."[10] A reconciled sinner shows evidence of divine work in his life by proper doctrinal belief. Any denial of the deity and redemptive work of Christ, subsequent to profession, demonstrates that the sinner did not genuinely accept Christ with essential understanding (Matt. 13:23).

The fact that the Colossians remained upon (epi) the faith is seen in three ways. Actually, the phrase "the faith" (tēi pistei) refers to that body of biblical truth which is essential to the doctrine of salvation, not to one's personal faith (Jude 3). Again, the issue is doctrinal accuracy, not gross sins such as immorality or murder. *First*, the Colossians were "grounded" (tethemeliōmenoi).[11] They had built a permanent spiritual foundation upon the person and work of Christ, as expounded by the apostles and prophets (I Cor. 3:11; Eph. 2:20). In the Sermon on the Mount, Christ spoke of people who build on a firm foundation:

> Therefore whosoever heareth these sayings of mine, and doeth them, I will liken him unto a wise man, which built his house upon a rock:

---

[10]There are four types of Greek conditional clauses. This is a conditional clause of the first class—"if" (ei) with the indicative mood ("continue," epimenete). The same type is used later (3:1).

[11]Perfect passive participle, used as a verbal adjective.

And the rain descended, and the floods came, and the winds blew, and beat upon that house; and it fell not: for it was founded upon a rock (Matt. 7:24–25).

Second, the Colossians were "settled" *(hedraioi).* This adjective denotes a strong superstructure, strengthened by the indwelling ministry of the Holy Spirit (Eph. 2:21–22).

Third, the Colossians were not being "moved away from the hope of the gospel" (cf. 1:4–5). The heretics tried to weaken their doctrinal convictions about the person of Christ and His work in creation and redemption, but the walls and footings of their faith did not develop any cracks. Paul warned elsewhere about such attacks: "That we henceforth be no more children, tossed to and fro, and carried about with every wind of doctrine, by the sleight of men, and cunning craftiness, whereby they lie in wait to deceive" (Eph. 4:14). Growth and production of spiritual fruit are the best safeguards (1:6). The best defense is a strong offense (Eph. 4:15; II Peter 1:10).

II. THE PURPOSE OF THE APOSTLE (1:23b–29)

The mention of "the gospel" serves as a transition from the work of God in the Colossian believers to the work of God through Paul. Three observations about the gospel are briefly introduced. *First,* the Colossians "heard" it from Epaphras or one of Paul's other associates.[12] *Second,* the same gospel "was preached to every creature which is under heaven." This idiom refers to the inhabited Roman world. It does not imply that every living person had heard the gospel, but that the same gospel which was preached to the Colossians was preached elsewhere, in all countries and to all classes of people: Jews and Gentiles, bond and free, rich and poor, male and female (cf. 3:11). On the other hand, the heresy at Colosse was a local phenomenon. *Third,* Paul

---

[12]The relative neuter pronoun "which" *(hou)* refers to "gospel," not to the feminine noun "hope."

became or was "made" *(egenomēn)* a minister of that gospel by divine selection and enablement (I Tim. 1:11–12).

The insertion of the emphatic personal words, "I Paul," serves as an introduction to his ministry in three areas.

A. Minister of the Gospel (1:23b)

Paul was an apostle, and yet he was also a "minister" *(diakonos)*. He twice makes this claim in this section (1:23, 25).

The word "minister" has both a technical and a general meaning. The former refers to an official position in the local church, an assistant to the pastor (Acts 6:1–7; I Tim. 3:8–13). The latter includes the ministry of angels (Matt. 4:11; Heb. 1:14), of women in giving and food preparation (Matt. 8:15; Mark 15:40–41), of Christ in His death (Matt. 20:28), and of preachers (I Cor. 3:5).

As a minister of the gospel, Paul was concerned about *what he preached*. This included doctrinal facts and truths.

B. Minister of the Church (1:24–27)

As a minister of the church, the emphasis is upon *whom Paul served* (1:25).[13] He was interested in people: in evangelizing them and in edifying them (I Cor. 9:19–23). He thus had three major concerns.

1. To suffer for the church (1:24)

At the time Paul wrote the epistle, he was a prisoner in Rome ("now," 4:3, 18). Despite this difficulty, he accomplished two goals. *First,* he rejoiced in his sufferings for the *local church* at Colosse ("for you"). He saw himself as its representative as he stood before pagan authorities because of false Jewish accusations. He was a prisoner because he preached the gospel of grace to uncircumcised Gentiles and incurred the wrath of Jewish religious leaders for doing so. He resisted both Jewish legalism and worldly philosophy. He rejoiced that he could do so. His "sufferings"

[13]The word "whereof" (v. 25) can also be translated "of which" *(hēs)*. It is a feminine relative pronoun referring back to its feminine antecedent "church."

(pathēmasi) were many and extreme (II Cor. 11:23—12:10). He suffered "in the defence and confirmation" of the very gospel which the Colossians heard (Phil. 1:7). If they would yield to the pressures of the heretics, then his suffering would have been in vain (cf. Gal. 4:10–11).

Second, Paul filled up "that which is behind of the afflictions of Christ in my flesh for his body's sake, which is the church." He thus suffered for the *universal church*. The verb *(antanaplērō)* means "to fill up in the place of." Paul was Christ's substitute. Christ suffered in death to save the church, and now Paul suffered in life to spare it. The redemptive work was finished at the cross, so Paul could add nothing to that accomplishment. In fact, the word "afflictions" *(thlipseōn)* is never used to describe the sufferings of Christ on the cross.

Christ said concerning Paul: "For I will shew him how great things he must suffer for my name's sake" (Acts 9:16). The apostle counted it a privilege to suffer for Him whom he once hated (Acts 9:4). Paul underwent great tribulation in the defense of the spiritual oneness of both Jew and Gentile in Christ.

2. To serve the church (1:25)

Paul had three relationships to the church. *First*, he was its "minister." He evangelized sinners, established local churches, trained their leaders, prayed for them, visited them, sent associates to them, and wrote epistles to them. He required no direct financial assistance for these labors. He did everything he could to seek the church's spiritual welfare.

Second, he was the church's steward. He conducted his ministry "according to the dispensation of God which is given to me for you." The word "dispensation" *(oikonomian)* literally means "house law." In every house, there are distinctive family rules. In every country or state, there are laws which pertain to what happens within its borders. In like manner, God has administered His redemptive program in different ways within the various ages of biblical history. He dealt with Adam differently after sin occurred than before his fall. After the Mosaic law was given, the people of Israel had more responsibilities before God than prior to that event. The crucifixion and resurrection of Christ likewise have changed the means of divine government in this age. These various periods can be called dispensations in that God revealed more truth and held men responsible to act according to this new revelation. In this age, God has produced out of believing Jews and Gentiles a new entity, the church. God imparted more truth about this unique age to Paul, especially as it pertained to the salvation and spiritual position of Gentiles. Paul saw himself as the main apostle and minister to the Gentile world ("to me for you"; Rom. 15:16; Gal. 2:7–9).

Third, Paul became the church's minister "to fulfil the word of God." In a primary sense, this means that he attempted to preach the truth of Gentile salvation by grace through faith throughout the known world (Rom. 15:14–21). In a secondary sense, it includes the inscripturated exposition of the revelation of distinctive church truth.

3. *To reveal the church (1:26–27)*

Paul revealed five concepts about the church. *First,* it is a "mystery" *(mustērion).*[14] This word is based on an ancient term which conveyed the idea of shutting the mouth. The biblical use carries the sense that "what was once silent is now vocal." Scriptural mysteries are divine truths once unknown and unspoken by men in past ages, but now proclaimed and understood by yielded believers (cf. I Cor. 2:7; 15:51). In this passage, the term is used in apposition to "the word of God," the concept of Gentile salvation within the true church (1:27).

Second, the essence of the church was "hid from ages and from generations" (cf. Eph. 3:5). The first term, "ages" *(aiōnōn),* refers to time periods; the second word, "generations" *(geneōn),* refers to the people who lived in those days. It would include both Jews and Gentiles, both the saved and the lost.

Third, this mystery "now is made manifest to his saints." The adverb "now" *(nuni)* contemplates the present church dispensation, with special application to the apostolic period when the

---

[14]This word is used twenty-seven times: three times in the Gospels; twenty times in Paul's letters; and four times in Revelation.

THE WORK OF GOD AND MAN

New Testament writings came into being. Elsewhere Paul wrote:

> How that by revelation he made known unto me the mystery; (as I wrote afore in few words,
>
> Whereby, when ye read, ye may understand my knowledge in the mystery of Christ)
>
> Which in other ages was not made known unto the sons of men, as it is now revealed unto his holy apostles and prophets by the Spirit (Eph. 3:3–5).

Fourth, the essence of the church was the object of divine revelation. The phrase literally reads, "To whom God willed to make known." God chose to create the church and to delay its revelation until the gospel-apostolic period. He had to do so because the mystery "from the beginning of the world hath been hid in God" (Eph. 3:9). The "riches of the glory of this mystery" are equivalent to the unsearchable riches of Christ. They envelop the total significance of His incarnation, crucifixion, resurrection, ascension, and the descent of the Holy Spirit.

Fifth, the "mystery among the Gentiles" is "Christ in you, the hope of glory." The Old Testament both depicted and predicted Gentile salvation through faith in the redeeming God of Israel, but it never revealed that Jews and Gentiles would become spiritually one in Christ and that Christ would dwell in believing Gentiles. Elsewhere, Paul wrote that the mystery is "that the Gentiles should be fellowheirs, and of the same body, and partakers of his promise in Christ by the gospel" (Eph. 3:6). Israel knew that the Messiah would dwell within her, but that He would abide in Gentiles was totally foreign to her comprehension. Christ predicted this mystical union: "At that day ye shall know that I am in my Father, and ye in me, and I in you" (John 14:20).

The Gnostic heretics constantly bragged about their spiritual knowledge which was inaccessible to the majority; however, all saints in this age can know what was heretofore unknown to the best minds of the past. The best mystery is a revealed mystery. It is not what we know that counts, but who we are and whom we have, namely, Christ.

C. Minister of Christ (1:28–29)

Paul belonged to Christ. He knew and lived that truth. He often identified himself as an apostle, prisoner, and minister of Christ (1:1; Rom. 15:16; Eph. 3:1). In his service, he wanted to accomplish three goals.

1. To preach Christ (1:28a)

Paul proclaimed a message which centered in a person ("whom we preach").[15] The present tense of the verb (*kataggellomen*) indicates the constant activity of the apostle and his associates. Christ was in his life and on his lips (Phil. 1:21). To preach the Word properly is to expound the person and redemptive work of the Savior (II Tim. 4:2). The Scriptures testify of Him (Luke 24:44–45; John 5:39; Rev. 19:10).

There were two aspects to Paul's proclamation: negative and positive. *First*, he was "warning every man." He admonished believers to watch for false teachers who would invade the church from outside and who would rise up within their ranks (Acts 20:29–31; Phil. 3:1–2). All parents, both physical and spiritual, should bring up their children "in the nurture and admonition [same word] of the Lord" (Eph. 6:4).

Second, Paul was "teaching every man." Instruction in creed and conduct is vital to Christian health. Believers must be taught what to believe and how to live. Didactic preaching is part of the discipleship program (Matt. 28:18–20).

The *sphere* of warning and teaching is "in all wisdom." That wisdom is redemptive and spiritual in character, and is found in Christ as revealed in history and in the Scriptures (2:3).

The *object* of Paul's ministry was every believer ("every man"). The double usage of this phrase shows that no believer, regardless of sex, race, or social strata, is excluded from the teaching ministry of the Holy Spirit through spiritual men. On the other hand, the heretics practiced an intellectual exclusivism.

---

[15]The pronoun "we" (*hēmeis*) is emphatic.

2. To present believers to Christ (1:28b)

Through his double ministry, the apostle wanted to "present every man perfect in Christ Jesus." Four concepts are found in this purpose clause introduced by "that" *(hina)*. *First*, the *agent* of presentation is man, whereas an earlier presentation was made by God (1:22). Paul desired that all believers present themselves to the Lord Jesus Christ to live for Him (Rom. 12:1–2), but here he wanted to present them, probably at the return of Christ. Elsewhere he wrote: "For I am jealous over you with godly jealousy: for I have espoused you to one husband, that I may present you as a chaste virgin to Christ" (II Cor. 11:2). The presentation by God deals with the position of a Christian, whereas the human presentation deals with the practice of a believer.

Second, the *object* of presentation is again "every man." This third usage in the same verse shows that Paul ministered to the total church congregation.

Third, the *goal* of presentation is perfection. All believers are presently "perfect" *(teleion)* or complete (2:10); in spiritual standing they are as complete as they can possibly be. All believers, however, are not yet perfect in their practice, the outworking of their acceptable position before God. Even Paul recognized that he could improve (Phil. 3:12). The word "perfect" speaks of the end or goal of a process.[16] The Gnostics used the term to describe one who had been fully initiated into the mystery cults, in contrast to a novice within their movement.

Fourth, the *sphere* of presentation is "in Christ Jesus." No ministry which ignores a true biblical Christology is worthy to be called a Christian ministry.

3. To labor by Christ's enablement (1:29)

The connective "whereunto" shows Paul's determination to accomplish his purpose. The word literally means "into which" *(eis ho)*.

[16]The word *telescope* is based upon it.

Three points should be made about Paul's effort. *First*, he labored *(kopiō)*. This word stresses physical and mental exhaustion, weariness, and toil. He put forth more effort than any other apostle (I Cor. 15:10). He labored night and day, preaching and making tents in order to support his ministry (I Thess. 2:9). He did that because he knew that his labor was "not in vain in the Lord" (I Cor. 15:58).

Second, Paul agonized or strove ("striving," *agōnizomenos*). This metaphor, taken from the terminology of wrestling, indicates the opposition which he faced in the pursuit of his task. In a weak, tired body, he still had to fight against satanic onslaughts (Eph. 6:12). At the end of his life, he could confidently affirm: "I have fought a good fight [same word]" (II Tim. 4:7). He achieved this only through divine enablement ("according to his working").

Third, God actually did the work in and through Paul ("which worketh in me mightily"). Paul did not originate the work and then ask God to relieve him when he grew tired. The ministry is a divine-human endeavor. Paul surrendered his availability to God's ability. In so doing, he paradoxically grew stronger as he became weaker (II Cor. 4:16; 12:10).

Questions for Discussion

1. How can men who deny the deity of Christ actually appear to be evangelical? How can their true doctrinal position be detected?

2. Is the blood of Christ still emphasized in preaching and singing today? Are there any acceptable words which can be substituted for "blood"?

3. In what ways do the unsaved manifest mental hostility toward God? How can it be seen in their lives?

4. Why do many groups insist that a believer can lose his salvation? What passages or concepts do they use?

5. Do evangelicals emphasize the local church today at the expense of the universal church? Is the opposite true? How can balance be maintained?

6. What other New Testament mysteries were hidden from past ages? What does progressive revelation mean to you?

7. Are some Christians overworked? Are others lazy? What can be done to achieve the biblical standard? What is that standard?

The Means of Perfection
Colossians 2:1–8

Gifted men, such as apostles, prophets, evangelists, and pastor-teachers, have been given to the church:

> For the perfecting of the saints, for the work of the ministry, for the edifying of the body of Christ:
> Till we all come in the unity of the faith, and of the knowledge of the Son of God, unto a perfect man, unto the measure of the stature of the fulness of Christ (Eph. 4:12–13).

No believer is independent of outside help in his determination to achieve spiritual perfection in this life. This pursuit is not optional; it is obligatory. Christ commanded: "Be ye therefore perfect, even as your Father which is in heaven is perfect" (Matt. 5:48).

Paul had already expressed his desire to "present every man perfect in Christ Jesus" (1:28). He not only desired to do so, but he had also put forth great effort (1:29). His labor involved both warning and teaching (1:28). The connective "for" *(gar)* introduces a further explanation of those two means. If he could achieve his goal in the Colossians' lives, they would attain their own mark of perfection.

I. THE TEACHING OF PAUL (2:1–3)

Spiritual teaching should always be warm and personal; it should never become cold, academic, and merely professional. It must be done with the heart as well as the head. The teacher must not only love *what* he is teaching, but *whom* he is teaching. The great apostle, whose teaching excelled in biblical content and logic, taught with his total being. Paul could say with unashamed frankness: "So being affectionately desirous of you, we were willing to have imparted unto you, not the gospel of God only, but also our own souls, because ye were dear unto us" (I Thess. 2:8).

A. Concern in Teaching (2:1)

1. Statement of concern

Believers should be informed that other Christians are interested in their spiritual welfare. Paul wanted the Colossians to know about his concern for them: "For I would that ye knew what great conflict I have for you . . . ."

The Colossians came to know Paul's concern through two basic means: the content of the epistle and the personal testimonies of Tychicus and Onesimus (4:7–9). They thus had the confirmation of at least two witnesses. They had the corroboration of the written word in the book and the spoken word from the two associates.

Three descriptions of the concern are given. *First*, it was a "conflict" *(agōna)*. Transliterated as "agony," this is the noun form of the verb "striving" *(agōnizomenos;* 1:29). What was general is now particular. Paul was concerned for all believers, and he was concerned for each believer.

Second, it was a "great" *(hēlikon)* concern. This word, used only twice in the New Testament, stresses magnitude. James observed: "Behold, how great [same word] a matter a little fire kindleth" (James 3:5). A raging forest fire which can devastate thousands of acres of timber can be started from a tiny spark. The report of the presence of heresy at Colosse caused the apostle to have abundant inner distress about the local church. Parents have natural concern when their children are still living at home, but parental anxiety increases when the children are miles away without any possibility of direct help or supervision. The same can be said of Paul's attitude toward the Colossians.

Third, this concern was constant. The present verb ("I have") points out continuity of interest. Even after Paul's associates left with the epistle, his concern persisted. He continued to wage spiritual battles through intercessory prayer and vicarious sufferings (1:24).

2. Areas of concern

Three groups of people are cited. *First*, Paul had concern for the believers at Colosse ("for you"). He earlier described them as "saints and faithful brethren" (1:2).

Second, Paul had concern "for them at Laodicea."[1] This city was located about forty miles southeast of Philadelphia on the road to Colosse. It was also situated on the Lycus River, about eleven miles west of Colosse. With Colosse and Hierapolis, it formed a unique area of three cities. The local congregation later became famous as one of the seven churches of Asia to which the Book of Revelation was sent (Rev. 1:4, 11; 3:14–22). It became a wealthy, fiercely self-sufficient group. The city is not mentioned by name outside of these two books. The church started as the direct result of Paul's evangelistic efforts in Ephesus (Acts 19:10). His associates probably traveled to Laodicea and won converts there. Because of its proximity to Colosse, Laodicea probably was invaded by the heretical teachers also. This explains, in part, why Paul commanded the Colossians to share their epistle with the Laodiceans (4:16). The church met in the house of Nymphas (4:15).

Third, Paul also had concern for "as many as have not seen my face in the flesh." This phrase had a primary reference to other believers in that region, including those at Hierapolis (4:13). As the apostle and spiritual father of the Roman province of Asia, he was interested in the lives of all Asian converts, both known and unknown to him. In a general sense, Paul loved the entire church, the family of God, even though he had not become personally acquainted with all of the members. The usage of the qualitative pronoun ("as many as") also includes the first two groups mentioned (cf. Acts 4:6; Rev. 18:17). He had not visited Colosse or Laodicea.

---

[1] The name means "judgment of the people."

THE MEANS OF PERFECTION

B. Purpose for Teaching (2:2)

The conjunction "that" *(hina)* shows the purpose behind Paul's concern and teaching. Although the entire verse enumerates one main goal, it can be divided into four separate aims. These four build upon each other.

1. To comfort

Paul desired that "their hearts might be comforted." The verb *(paraklēthōsin)* literally means "to be called beside." A comforter, therefore, is one who is called to stand beside another person (John 14:16, 26). This comfort can involve either consolation for the sorrowing or encouragement for the weak and perplexed. The Colossians needed the latter ministry. The Holy Spirit is the divine comforter who encourages through both the Scriptures (Rom. 15:4) and involved people; thus, the apostle sent Tychicus "that he might know your estate, and comfort your hearts" (4:8).

The heart *(kardiai)* refers to the total inner being of a person, with special attention to his thoughts and feelings (Prov. 23:7).

2. To unite

Everett F. Harrison correctly observed: "Because human understanding is so limited, truth sometimes divides; but love always unites."[2] The legalistic, intellectual error had caused schism within the congregation. The believers were fragmented in their evaluation of the new doctrine and in their relationship to the heretical teachers.

Paul wanted the believers to be "knit together in love." The verb *(sumbibasthentōn)* reflects a medical metaphor. It means "to join or unite together." Since believers are members of the spiritual body of Christ, they should not be out of joint. They should all be in submission to "the Head, from which all the body by joints and bands having nourishment ministered, and knit together [same word], increaseth with the increase of God" (2:19; cf. Eph. 4:16).

Organizational unity and conformity without love, however, are like lifeless bones joined together in a skeleton. The Colossians

[2] Everett F. Harrison, *Colossians: Christ All-sufficient*, p. 49.

had to be connected to each other "in love." Love is the blood stream of the body; it is "the bond of perfectness" which holds everything in place (3:14). This is love both for God and for each other. Defense of the truth without love produces hardness (Rev. 2:2–4).

3. To assure

Paul wanted the Colossians to attain "unto all riches of the full assurance of understanding." The essence of spiritual "understanding" *(suneseōs)* is the Spirit-guided ability to perceive the redemptive purpose of God in the Scriptures and to relate it to the complexities of contemporary life. He is able to integrate the so-called sacred and secular into a united whole.

Such understanding will produce an unmovable conviction of the heart ("full assurance"). This word *(plērophorias)* characterized Abraham's faith in the power and promise of God to give him a son (Rom. 4:21). The heretics had caused the Colossians to question their doctrinal foundations. They were forced to reexamine their understanding of the person of Christ and His work in creation and redemption. The apostle wanted them to know beyond a shadow of doubt that they were in the truth.

The greatest wealth ("unto all riches") is divinely imparted wisdom whereby a believer can say with ultimate confidence: "I know whom I have believed, and am persuaded that he is able to keep that which I have committed unto him against that day" (II Tim. 1:12). Christ depicted the poor church as Smyrna as rich, and the rich church at Laodicea as poor (Rev. 2:9; 3:17).

4. To inform

The final goal was "the acknowledgement of the mystery of God, and of the Father, and of Christ."[3] The mystery "is Christ, as incarnating the fulness of the Godhead, and all the divine wisdom and knowledge for the redemption and reconciliation of man."[4] It centers in the mystical union between Christ and the

[3] The critical Greek text ends the phrase in this way: ". . . the mystery of God, Christ." Christ is thus either in apposition to God or an explanation of the mystery.

[4] Scofield Reference Edition of the Bible, p. 1263.

body of believers within this church age (1:26–27). Elsewhere Paul wrote: "For we are members of his body, of his flesh, and of his bones . . . . This is a great mystery: but I speak concerning Christ and the church" (Eph. 5:30, 32).

The sense of "acknowledgement" (epignōsin; cf. 1:10) is a thorough comprehension of what God is doing today and how that relates to His program for the ages. It implies a full theological, dispensational, and Christological approach to life.

C. Content of Teaching (2:3)

1. Wisdom is in Christ

Genuine wisdom is centered in a person, not in facts written on paper. Thus Paul wrote: "In whom are hid all the treasures of wisdom and knowledge." The relative pronoun ("whom") links the content of this verse with "Christ," its antecedent.[5] True life is in knowing God through Christ (John 17:2).

Contemporary man, unfortunately, separates his religion from the rest of his life. But all truth, not some, resides in Christ. He is its center and circumference. The English term thesaurus is based upon the Greek word translated as "treasures" (thēsauroi). Spiritual wisdom is spiritual wealth.

The Gnostic teachers claimed that "knowledge" (gnōseōs) rested in them. Christ, however, is the real depository of true knowledge and wisdom. If knowledge refers to the understanding of each particular truth, then "wisdom" (sophia) sees the relationship between the truths. The former perceives truth in its parts, whereas the latter comprehends it in its whole (I Cor. 13:9).

2. Wisdom is hid

The predicate adjective "hid" (apokruphoi) is related to the verb "hidden" (apokekrummenon; 1:26). Just as the world "knew him not" when Christ lived on the earth, so sinful man cannot understand the real meaning of life or the redemptive program

---

[5]The pronoun (hōi) can be either masculine, referring to Christ, or neuter, referring to the mystery. Since the mystery centers in Christ, there is no major grammatical issue here.

recorded in the biblical record (John 1:10). It is hidden to those who are wise in their own sight (Matt. 11:25), to government authorities (I Cor. 2:6–8), and to the lost of all ages. However, such wisdom has been revealed to those who see themselves as spiritually ignorant babes (Matt. 11:25), to the saints of this age (1:26).

Since this treasure is in Christ, and Christ is in each believer, each child of God has full access to it. By inference, the heretical concept of a spiritual caste system is refuted. The believer, however, must actively study the Word of God in order to "grow in grace, and in the knowledge of our Lord and Savior Jesus Christ" (II Peter 3:18). The key to the treasure is yieldedness and cleanliness.

II. THE WARNING OF PAUL (2:4–8)

The opening words, "and this I say," form the transition between the two sections. They refer to the previous instruction (2:1–3) and anticipate the four warnings which follow. The first two warnings are introduced by the negative conjunction "lest" (2:4, 8) and the second two by prohibitions, "let no man" (2:16, 18).

A. Means of Error (2:4)

One germ can infect the entire body, and one drop of poison can pollute a cup of pure water. Paul recognized the threat of even one false teacher ("any man"). The indefinite pronoun *(tis)* shows that the apostle was far more concerned with the methods of deceit than with the identity of the deceiver. The principle, not the person, was the key. The singular usage, however, does not imply that only one false teacher had penetrated the Colossians' midst.

1. False teachers beguile

The verb "beguile" *(paralogizētai)* literally means "to reason or speak beside." Beguilement involves faulty logic which is not based upon the authoritative Word of God. It uses erroneous interpretations, giving meanings and making applications other than those which are normally accepted. In nonbiblical literature, the term denoted cheating by false reasoning. Paul warned against building upon a foundation that was placed beside Christ, rather than upon a proper doctrinal comprehension of His person and redemptive work (I Cor. 3:11). The word is used elsewhere only once: "But be ye doers of the word, and not hearers only, deceiving [same word] your own selves" (James 1:22). The illogical reasoning of the heretics at Colosse rested upon faulty premises and presuppositions, such as the evil character of matter, the denial of the Trinity, and the repudiation of the concept of the incarnation.

2. False teachers entice

False teachers attempt to beguile with "enticing words." These two words are actually the translation of a single Greek term (*pithanologia*) which depicts a type of speech which is designed to persuade others. In the papyri, the term was used of thieves who attempted to retain their booty by facile speech. It is what a crafty salesman uses to convince a person to buy something which he really does not want. It is error carefully packaged and presented.

Paul deplored such deceitful tactics: "And my speech and my preaching was not with enticing words of man's wisdom, but in demonstration of the Spirit and of power" (I Cor. 2:4). He did persuade men to accept Christ (Acts 18:4), but he did not use rational and emotional appeals which were devoid of biblical content or spiritual import.

B. Protection Against Error (2:5–7)

Believers must be alert. They should watch out for the enemy, but they should also build their defenses. When the walls of Jerusalem were rebuilt under the supervision of Nehemiah, the construction workers built with their swords beside them (Neh. 4:18).

1. Unity (2:5)

Unity can be real or false. Friends and relatives are often shocked when a "strong" marriage ends in divorce. Unity has both an outward and an inward character. It envelops how people see us and how we really are.

First, Paul praised the Colossian believers for their spiritual oneness. Epaphras reported that the church had advanced even though the threat of heresy was real. Paul accepted the testimony of this eyewitness as absolutely true and responded as if he had actually been in the city himself ("For though I be absent in the flesh, yet am I with you in the spirit"). He judged the fornicator at Corinth *in absentia* (I Cor. 5:3). He informed the young converts at Thessalonica that he was still with them "in heart," even though he was miles away in Achaia (I Thess. 2:17). In legal situations, the judge and the jury must base their conclusions upon the witness of others.

Paul's response to the report by Epaphras and to the situation at Colosse was twofold ("joying and beholding"). He reckoned himself to be a present observer and he rejoiced about what he saw. It is always an encouragement to Christians to go on in their faith when others tell them that they are noticed and appreciated.

Second, Paul described the Colossians' unity in two ways. First, they had "order" *(taxin)*. In the military world, orderly soldiers were those who had no breaks or breaches in their ranks. Each was in his assigned place and performed his duty. In the Jewish world, the term was used of the priestly orders of Aaron and of Melchisedec (Heb. 5:6; 7:11). This word conveys the idea that each priest carried out his own responsibilities in order that the goal of the entire priesthood would be fulfilled. A disorderly person, on the other hand, disobeys the clear commandments given to him (I Cor. 14:37, 40; II Thess. 3:6–11).

Second, the Colossians had "stedfastness." The emphasis of "order" is on individuality, but the focus of this word is on corporate strength. This noun *(stereōma)*[6] is found only here, but its adjective form is used of the "sure" foundation of God (II Tim. 2:19), the "strong" meat of the Scriptures (Heb. 5:12), and "stedfast" resistance to Satan (I Peter 5:9). The verb form *(stereoō)* re-

---

[6]The English *stereo,* as in *stereophonic* ("solid sound"), is based upon this word.

ferred to ankle bones made strong (Acts 3:7, 16) and to the establishment of churches in the faith (Acts 16:5). In warfare, it depicted the strength of a united front.

2. Walk (2:6–7)

Paul earlier prayed that the believers at Colosse might have a worthy walk, marked by fruitfulness, knowledge, strength, and thanksgiving (1:10–12). In Ephesians, written at the same time as Colossians, he charged those believers to walk worthy of their divine calling, not as the Gentiles, but in love, as children of light, and circumspectly (Eph. 4:1, 17; 5:2, 8, 15).

Now Paul issues a clear command for the believers to walk in Christ. The present tense of the verb *(peripateite)* stresses the daily walk of spiritual development. Six features of this walk are given. *First,* the Colossians were to walk "as [they] have therefore received Christ Jesus the Lord." The opening words, "as therefore" *(hōs oun),* form the transition and conclusion to the preceding verse where Paul mentioned their saving faith exercised at their conversion ("your faith in Christ"; 2:5). They received Him by faith; therefore, they should walk by faith (Rom. 1:17). The verb "received" *(parelabete)* refers to the time when Epaphras evangelized and taught them. Paul often used this word to describe the process of discipleship (Matt. 28:18–20; cf. I Cor. 15:1–3; Gal. 1:9; Phil. 4:9; I Thess. 2:13; 4:1; II Thess. 3:6). The title of the Savior, "Christ Jesus the Lord," is unique, occurring only here in Paul's letters.[7] It depicts the total doctrine of Christology which was under attack. The Colossians received a person, not a philosophy.

Second, the Colossians should walk "in him." As a fish swims and lives in water, so a believer must walk in Him. Christ Himself said: ". . . without me ye can do nothing" (John 15:5). The practice of the Christian should manifest his position in Him.

Third, the believers should be "rooted" *(errizōmenoi).* At conversion, they actually put their roots down deep into Him; now they should continue to draw their life and sustenance from

---

[7] Literally, "the Christ Jesus the Lord."

Him.[8] He must be the rich soil out of which they grow into fruitful Christians. The passive voice of the participle indicates that God placed the believer into Christ by the baptism in the Holy Spirit (I Cor. 12:13). In the only other New Testament usage of the verb, Paul asserted that genuine believers are "rooted and grounded in love" (Eph. 3:17).

Fourth, believers should be "built up in him." At conversion, all believing sinners were "built upon the foundation of the apostles and prophets, Jesus Christ himself being the chief corner stone" (Eph. 2:20).[9] The emphasis of regeneration is upon the proper foundation; however, the focus of spiritual growth is upon the superstructure. Elsewhere Paul cautioned that believers could use two different types of building materials in the formation of their lives: "gold, silver, precious stones, wood, hay, stubble" (I Cor. 3:10–12). The first three represent quality, value, permanence, a life lived for the glory of God; the second three symbolize hypocrisy, faulty motivations, and effort produced by the flesh. At the judgment seat of Christ, Christians will be evaluated on the intrinsic worth of their labor (I Cor. 3:13–15; II Cor. 5:10).

Fifth, the Colossians should be "stablished in the faith." It is not enough to place brick upon brick in a wall of support; bricks must be properly anchored and cemented to each other to provide inner strength. This is true for Christians, too—the sphere of stability and firmness is found "in the faith." This phrase includes the whole body of doctrinal truth which had been revealed through the apostles at that time (Jude 3). It involves content, fact, and the various divisions of theology. A person cannot obtain the necessary stability through his own inner faith or experience. Although God can teach a believer directly from his own inductive Bible study, He normally instructs through gifted teachers ("as ye have been taught"). The Colossians learned from Epaphras

[8] Suggested by the perfect passive participle. The next three participles in the verse are in the present tense, which stress the need for daily practice: "built up," "stablished," and "abounding."

[9] This is an aorist participle indicating that the action was done: *epoikodomē- thentes*.

(1:7). Paul outlined this procedure for doctrinal pedagogy: "And the things that thou hast heard of me among many witnesses, the same commit thou to faithful men, who shall be able to teach others also" (II Tim. 2:2). If a believer is to be taught in the faith, then the teacher himself must know what that faith is. In fact, the pastor-teacher has also been taught by someone else (Titus 1:9).

Sixth, the believers should walk "abounding therein with thanksgiving." The word "therein" is actually a prepositional phrase, "in it," *(en autēi)*, which refers back to "the faith" *(tēi pistei)*.[10] Instruction in biblical doctrine should produce inner joy and gratitude. The more believers learn about God and His redemptive program, the more they should love Him for what He has done for them.

C. Description of Error (2:8)

Believers should be on constant alert for the inroads of error ("Beware").[11] In a similar warning, the apostle cautioned: "Beware of dogs, beware of evil workers, beware of the concision" (Phil. 3:2). Since error is rarely separate from personality, Christians should watch out for men who bring a false message. The heretical messenger can be "any man" *(tis);* the indefiniteness of identity suggests that believers should scrutinize both fellow church members and itinerant preachers (Acts 20:29–31).

1. The goal of error

The heretic wants to "spoil" *(sulagōgōn)* the believer. This compound verb means "to lead or carry away *(agō)* booty" *(sulē)*.[12] Here, the force of the threat is not so much to rob the Christian of something as to kidnap him ("you"). The heretical teacher, therefore, is like a slave trader. He wants to steal the believer away from his spiritual family and sell him as a slave into false doctrine.

---

[10] Both the pronoun and its antecedent are in the feminine gender.

[11] Present active imperative: *blepete mē.*

[12] Used only here in the New Testament.

2. The features of error

The preposition "through" *(dia)* shows the means by which the heretics would attempt to capture the believers. Five features of this methodology are enumerated. *First*, it is "philosophy" *(philosophia)*. The term basically means a "love of wisdom." Paul was not against wisdom *per se;* rather, he opposed a specific type of philosophy. The Greek text reads *"the* philosophy" *(tēs philosophias)*. A mere love of wisdom for the sake of wisdom is wrong; this type of philosophy unfortunately is humanistic and manifests the wisdom of the world. A genuine philosophy is a love of wisdom which has its source and meaning in Christ (2:3). Paul encountered worldly philosophers at Athens where they mocked him for declaring the deity and redemptive work of Christ (Acts 17:18).

Second, this methodology employs "vain deceit" *(kenēs apatēs)*. If philosophy stresses *what* is taught, then deceit depicts *how* and *why* it is taught. These tactics constitute two aspects of the same error.[13] What is taught is "vain" *(kenēs)* or empty in that it contains no substance to edify. It is void of genuine spiritual truth, power, and hope.

Third, worldly philosophy is "after the tradition of men." Traditions *(paradosin)* can be either good (II Thess. 2:15; 3:6) or bad (Mark 7:3). Since the heretical traditions at Colosse originated with men and elevated a legalistic approach to God (2:21–22), they were innately evil.

Fourth, this methodology is "after the rudiments of the world." This old word *(stoicheia)* was used of anything which appeared in a row or a series; thus, it came to refer to the letters of the alphabet, to the basic notes of music, and to the fundamental components of the material universe (II Peter 3:10–12). In the context of heresy, Paul used it to describe legalistic observances, both Jewish and pagan (2:16–17, 20–22; Gal. 4:3, 9). In the Judaistic Gnostic heresy at Colosse, the term probably denoted the outline for the initial requirements of new converts. Such legal

---

[13] The Granville Sharp rule of grammar can be seen here: *dia tēs philosophias kai kenēs apatēs*. Following the preposition are two nouns introduced by one definite article and joined by "and."

conformity was the first step toward the ultimate denial of all which was accomplished at the cross.

Fifth, the methodology is "not after Christ." A Christian philosophy centers in Him and seeks to understand more fully His incarnate person and His redemptive death and resurrection.

Questions for Discussion

1. How can believers encourage and comfort each other? When should this occur?

2. How can unity be achieved in the midst of denominational diversity? What is the common basis for genuine unity?

3. What enticing words can be seen today in various sects and cults? How does brainwashing fit into this?

4. In what ways do Christians walk in a disorderly manner? How can true spiritual compliance be achieved?

5. How can believers indeed walk by faith? Why is there a tendency to walk by sight?

6. What false philosophies are prevalent today? How can their deceitfulness be detected?

7. How has legalism infiltrated evangelicalism? Give examples. How can this be corrected?

The Identification with Christ
Colossians 2:9–15

One of the meanings of "identification" is "the condition of being the same as something else." In the spiritual life, proper identification occurs when the believer confesses: "Not I, but Christ" (Gal. 2:20). Paul has already expounded on the mystery of the mystical union. Christ is in the child of God, and the Christian is in Him (1:14, 27–28).

A proper understanding of this identification of the believer with Christ will promote the triumphant life of godliness and will protect the believer against non-Christian intellectualism and oppressive legalism. In this section of the epistle, Paul further delineated the advantages of being in Christ.

I. IN HIS PERSON (2:9–10)

The connective "for" (hoti) indicates the reason why believers should beware of a philosophy which is not after Christ (2:8). He alone is the standard by which all religious claims must be judged.

A. The Fullness of God in Christ (2:9)

1. Its meaning

Earlier, the apostle declared that "it pleased the Father that in [Christ] should all fulness dwell" (1:19). Now, he repeats the same truth but with a significant addition: "For in him dwelleth all the fulness of the Godhead bodily."

First, the inclusive phrase, "all the fulness" *(pan to plērōma),* denotes all that God is in His divine essence. It envelops the totality of the divine characteristics. John attributed full deity to Jesus Christ when he carefully asserted that "the Word was God" (John 1:1). The Son is neither the Father nor the Spirit, but all three persons within the trinitarian distinction are equally God. This deity could never be diminished or lost. God can never be less than what He is (Mal. 3:10; James 1:17). Even on earth, Christ declared: "I and my Father are one" (John 10:30). The explicit nature of the divine fullness is further claimed by the qualifying words "all" and "the."

Second, Christ possesses the fullness "of the Godhead" *(tēs theotētos).* This noun, found only here in the New Testament, is based upon the Greek word for "God" *(theos).* Another word *(theiotēs)* is translated as "Godhead," but there is a subtle theological difference. In his demonstration that the entire world is guilty before God, Paul argued: "For the invisible things of him from the creation of the world are clearly seen, being understood by the things that are made, even his eternal power and Godhead; so that they are without excuse" (Rom. 1:20). This latter term is derived from an adjective *(theios),* translated as "divine" (Acts 17:29; II Peter 1:3–4).

Nature reveals God *as He acts,* but Christ revealed God *as He is* (John 1:18). Since God is a personal being, He cannot be known personally through things. The natural creation can show that God exists and that He is intelligent and powerful, but only Christ could manifest the fact that God is loving, merciful, and forgiving. A person can learn about God through nature, but he can know God only through the incarnate Son (John 14:9).

Some scholars suggest that *theotētos* (2:9) refers to the essence of God, to deity, and to His Godhead, whereas *theiotēs* (Rom. 1:20) denotes the attributes of God, His divinity, and His Godhood.

2. *Its location*

The sphere of divine fullness is seen in two ways. *First,* it is "in him." The antecedent of the personal pronoun is definitely "Christ" (2:8). The emphatic position of the prepositional phrase reinforces the concept that only in Christ could the essence of deity dwell bodily.[1]

Second, the divine fullness is in Christ "bodily" *(sōmatikōs).* As God the eternal Son, Christ always possessed the fullness of the Godhead. The apostle earlier established the fact that He existed as God before the worlds began (1:15–17). In refutation of the heretical teaching that matter is intrinsically evil, Paul now asserts that Christ was still God, in the fullest sense of the word, even after the incarnation. There was no loss or corruption of the divine essence when the eternal Son took to Himself a full and complete humanity. In fact, the crucifixion, resurrection, and subsequent exaltation of Christ did not alter the hypostatic union. Although a surrender and a restoration of divine glory occurred at the incarnation and resurrection respectively (John 17:5), this truth did not affect the innate possession of deity by the Son of God.

3. Its permanence

When Paul wrote this epistle, Christ had been in the third heaven (the presence of God) for almost thirty years. The usage of the present tense of the verb "dwelleth" *(katoikei)* thus points out two facts about Christ. *First,* He still had a material body—a resurrected, immortal, incorruptible body—which could be seen and touched. The incarnation presupposes a permanent union between the divine and the human natures in Christ. He did not surrender His deity at His incarnation, and He did not give up His humanity at His resurrection.

Second, the verb denotes permanent residency in contrast to a temporary sojourn *(paroikeō).* As God the Son, Christ shared equally in the essence of deity. When He became man, this fullness came to indwell a human nature (1:19; aorist *katoikēsai*) and presently abides in His divine-human person.

---

[1] It occurs before the verb both in the English and Greek texts.

B. The Completeness of the Believer in Christ (2:10)

The simple connective ("and") serves to join the ideas that the fullness of God is in Christ and the believer is complete in Christ. The two key words of this section, "fulness" *(plērōma)* and "complete" *(peplērōmenoi)*, both come from the same Greek verbal stem *(plēroō)*. Both Christ and the Christian have fullness, but for different reasons.

1. Its meaning

All believers "are complete" in Christ. The concept behind this verb construction is that they became complete in the Savior at conversion and that they presently stand in a position of total spiritual completeness before God.[2] In fact, the main emphasis is upon the continuity of their acceptable stance ("ye are"). The passive voice of the verb shows that God completed believers through the ministry of the Holy Spirit who applied the positional benefits of Christ's redemptive work to them. They did not complete themselves through intense self-effort. Their position, not their practice, is in view. In Christ, they were complete. The heretics promoted a spiritual caste system whereby an adherent could become more complete as he achieved certain goals. But Paul emphasized that a total completeness is the possession of all believers.

The word *completeness* was used of a ship, totally fitted and ready for a voyage. The first man lost his moral, mental, and spiritual completeness at his fall in the Garden of Eden, but the regenerate man has regained it in Christ (3:10). John commented: "And of his fulness *(plērōmatos)* have all we received, and grace for grace" (John 1:16). This fulness has been specially applied to "the church, which is his body, the fulness of him that filleth all in all" (Eph. 1:23).

Everett F. Harrison observed that "in the Savior all the potential of the redeemed life lies accessible and can be communicated,

---

[2]This is a periphrastic usage of the perfect passive participle with the present indicative: *este peplērōmenoi*.

as faith draws upon Him."[3] In that sense, Paul prayed that all saints "might be filled with all the fulness of God" (Eph. 3:19) and that they might mature "unto the measure of the stature of the fulness of Christ" (Eph. 4:13).

2. Its location

The sphere of completeness is only in Christ ("in him"). Actually, His realm is emphasized as seen in this literal translation: "And you are in him complete" *(kai este en autōi peplērōmenoi).*

The significance of this spiritual location is reinforced by this personal identification: ". . . which is the head of all principality and power." Since Christ created all celestial beings, both good and evil, they are all subject to His sovereign rule (1:15–16).[4] The heretics charged that an angelic pleroma ruled over the world of men, but the believer shares in Christ's headship over the created universe through his completeness in the Savior. Such completeness gives a Christian direct and personal access to the Father; he does not have to work his way back through angelic intermediaries and legal conformity, as the Gnostics instructed.

II. IN HIS POWER (2:11–15)

The emphasis in the first part of this section was upon who Christ is, but in the second half, it is upon what He has done. The believer thus can identify himself with His redemptive work as well as with His redeeming person. Five areas of work can be detected.

A. Circumcision (2:11)

The opening prepositional phrase ("in whom also") serves to join the two sections. The position of the believer in Christ is what guarantees to him all spiritual blessings (Eph. 1:3).

---

[3] Everett F. Harrison, *Colossians: Christ All-sufficient,* p. 59.

[4] All angels were created good (Gen. 1:31), but some became evil when they followed Lucifer in his willful rebellion.

THE IDENTIFICATION WITH CHRIST

1. The fact

The Colossians literally were "circumcised" *(perietmēthēte)*.[5] The word means "to cut around." The rite was first practiced when Abraham circumcised Ishmael, his household servants, and himself in direct obedience to the command of God (Gen. 17:9–14; cf. 17:23–27). From that point on, all physical descendants of Abraham were circumcised at the age of eight days to show faith in the fulfillment of the promises contained in the Abrahamic covenant (Gen. 17:1–10). In time, the rite developed into a distinctive racial barrier between Jew and Gentile (3:11). The Gentiles became known as the "Uncircumcision," whereas the Jews identified themselves as the "Circumcision" (Eph. 2:11).

Some of the Jews who professed Christianity believed that physical circumcision was essential to salvation and tried to force that rite upon converted Gentiles (Acts 15:1; Gal. 6:12). At Colosse, the heretics sought to impose circumcision as an initiatory rite to their brand of Christianity.

All believers, however, were circumcised spiritually when they were converted. Positional circumcision, not physical, is what the apostle had in view: "For we are the circumcision, which worship God in the spirit, and rejoice in Christ Jesus, and have no confidence in the flesh" (Phil. 3:3).

2. The type

It is "the circumcision made without hands" *(peritomēi acheiropoiētōi)* which saves. The Jews unfortunately equated outward conformity with inward reality, but Paul dispelled that faulty logic: "For he is not a Jew, which is one outwardly; neither is that circumcision, which is outward in the flesh: But he is a Jew, which is one inwardly; and circumcision is that of the heart, in the spirit, and not in the letter" (Rom. 2:28–29). Even the Old Testament prophets cried out for Israel to repent and to circumcise their hearts (Deut. 10:16; 30:6; Jer. 4:4; 9:26). Stephen declared that the circumcised Jews were "stiffnecked and uncircumcised in heart and ears" (Acts 7:51).

---

[5] Aorist passive indicative.

3. The result

Inner, spiritual circumcision results "in putting off the body of the sins of the flesh."[6] This action occurs at conversion and removes the guilt, penalty, and pollution of the sin principle with its sinful thoughts and deeds. It does not eradicate the sin nature, but it does strip away the power of the sin nature so that a believer does not need to obey its dictates anymore. It is equivalent to the action of "[putting] off [*apekdusamenoi;* same word] the old man with his deeds" (3:9). The same word is translated "spoiled" in the later reference to Christ's triumph over evil angels at His resurrection (2:15).

4. The means

Spiritual circumcision is made possible "by the circumcision of Christ." This statement does not mean that the believer was in Christ when the infant Jesus was physically circumcised when He was eight days old (Luke 2:21). Rather, Christ is the one who circumcises the inner man.[7] He performs this spiritual ministry at the time of the conversion of the sinner when He applies the benefits of His death and resurrection.

B. Baptism (2:12)

The initiatory rite into Judaism is circumcision, but the introductory ordinance of organized Christendom is water baptism (Matt. 28:18–20; Acts 2:41). Water baptism, however, is only an outward sign of an inner work of grace. Unfortunately, many professing Christians have put their confidence in this external sign as the means of their salvation.

Several types of baptism are mentioned in the New Testament: Judaistic ceremonial cleansings (Heb. 6:2), the baptism of repentance by John the Baptist, which anticipated the establishment of the kingdom (Matt. 3:2; Luke 3:3), the personal baptism of Jesus Christ (Matt. 3:13–17), the baptism of suffering at the cross (Matt. 20:22–23), the baptism in the Holy Spirit (Acts 1:5; I Cor.

---

[6]The critical Greek text omits the words "the sins of."

[7]The genitive "of Christ" is thus seen as a subjective genitive.

12:13), and Christian water baptism in which the believer identifies himself with Christ in His death, burial, and resurrection.

Which baptism is expounded in this verse? There is no indication that the believer was in Christ when He was baptized in the Jordan River. The converts of John the Baptist later submitted to Christian baptism (Acts 19:1–7). Since spiritual circumcision, without human hands, has just been explained (2:11), this must be spiritual baptism, the "one baptism" which unites believers with each other in the body of Christ, the true church, and with Christ the living Head. Ceremonies performed by men can never achieve eternal redemption. This is one of the reasons why Paul attacked the heretical, legalistic approach to God at Colosse.

1. Baptism involves burial

Believers were "buried with him in baptism." Burial presupposes death. When Jesus Christ died on the cross and was buried in the tomb, all believers were spiritually identified with Him in those acts. The phrase "in baptism" literally reads "in the baptism" *(en tōi baptismati)*. The definite article "the" points out the one true baptism in the Holy Spirit which all believers received at their conversion (I Cor. 12:13; Eph. 4:5).

Elsewhere, the apostle explained:

Know ye not, that so many of us as were baptized into Jesus Christ were baptized into his death?

Therefore we are buried with him by baptism into death: that like as Christ was raised up from the dead by the glory of the Father, even so we also should walk in newness of life.

For if we have been planted together in the likeness of his death, we shall be also in the likeness of his resurrection (Rom. 6:3–5).

Since the believer is in Christ, God reckons the death and resurrection of Christ to be that of the child of God. Just as sin and death do not have dominion over Him, neither do they have dominion over the Christian. The believer needs to believe this truth and to apply this positional reality to his practical experience: "Likewise reckon ye also yourselves to be dead indeed unto sin, but alive unto God through Jesus Christ our Lord" (Rom. 6:11).

2. Baptism involves resurrection

Believers were also raised with Christ *(sunēgerthēte)*. In the judicial sense, this occurred at the actual physical resurrection of Christ, but it is spiritually realized at regeneration. The connective "wherein" *(en hōi)* can refer either to Christ or to the baptism, probably the latter in order to keep the analogy consistent.

Although water baptism by immersion best pictures the procedure of death, burial, and resurrection, it is not the means to secure that form of identification with Christ. Being raised with Christ comes "through the faith of the operation of God, who hath raised him from the dead." In order to experience deliverance from both physical and spiritual death, a person must believe that God has raised Christ from the dead and that He will deliver the believing sinner from eternal, spiritual death. Herbert M. Carson correctly observed: "The mighty working of God as already demonstrated in the resurrection of Christ is thus the object of the believer's confidence."[8]

C. Quickening (2:13)

1. The need for quickening

The emphasis here is upon the spiritual plight of the Colossians at the time of their conversion ("and you").[9] The present participle "being" *(ontas)* shows that their condition was constant and unchanging.

The Colossians were "dead" *(nekrous)*. They had no spiritual life; they were "alienated from the life of God through the ignorance that is in them, because of the blindness of their heart" (Eph. 4:18). They were alive physically, but dead spiritually. Christ came into the world to give such people life (John 10:10). This metaphorical usage of the adjective must be related to its normal physical meaning. Christ was raised from the realm of the dead ones *(nekrōn; 2:12)*. Physical death occurs when the human

---

[8] Herbert M. Carson, *The Epistles of Paul to the Colossians and to Philemon*, p. 67.

[9] The direct object "you," *(humas)* stands first in the sentence.

spirit is separated from the body, but all men begin their existence in a state of separation from God.

The Colossians were dead in two realms. *First*, they were dead in "sins" *(paraptōmasi)*. This compound word is based upon the verb "to fall" *(piptō)* and the preposition "beside" *(para)*. It denotes deliberate acts of sin in which a person chooses to deviate from the path of righteousness. It is often translated as "trespasses" (2:13; Eph. 2:1). Though they had no knowledge of the Mosaic law, pagan Gentiles nevertheless still had a sense of moral oughtness in their consciences—which they continued to violate (Rom. 2:14–15).

Second, the Colossians were dead in "the uncircumcision of their flesh." This expression could refer to the fact that they had not yet been spiritually circumcised by Christ (2:11). However, this unique term *(akrobustia)*, which literally meant "the foreskin of the penis," normally designated the pagan Gentile world. They were uncircumcised both racially and redemptively. Paul observed:

> Wherefore remember, that ye being in time past Gentiles in the flesh, who are called Uncircumcision by that which is called the Circumcision in the flesh made by hands;
>
> That at that time ye were without Christ, being aliens from the commonwealth of Israel, and strangers from the covenants of promise, having no hope, and without God in the world (Eph. 2:11–12).

Their sins and their race separated them from both God and God's covenant people. They were indeed dead.

2. *Its means*

God "quickened together with him" all believing sinners. The verb *(sunezōopoiēse)* means "to make alive with." Positionally, when God raised Christ from the physical dead, He also raised spiritually the believing sinner. In personal experience, the truth becomes actual at the time of saving faith. Elsewhere Paul wrote: "Even when we were dead in sins, hath [God] quickened us together with Christ, (by grace ye are saved;) And hath raised us up together, and made us sit together in heavenly places in Christ

Jesus" (Eph. 2:5–6). The sinner is made alive through the ministry of the Holy Spirit who convicts through the Word of God and
energizes him to believe unto life everlasting.

3. Its result

There can be no spiritual life apart from forgiveness. In the divine order, forgiveness precedes quickening.[10] The verbal action
of forgiveness (charisamenos) stems from the "grace" (charis) of
God. Forgiveness is totally undeserved; it is apart from human
merit. Sinners do not earn forgiveness; they receive it as a gracious gift of a merciful God.

The scope of forgiveness is "all trespasses." In providing reconciliation, God did not impute the trespasses of sinners to them
(II Cor. 5:19). That barrier to a proper return to a loving God was
removed at the cross, but actual forgiveness occurs at the time of
willful acceptance.

D. Removal of the Law (2:14)

Paul wrote that "the law is holy, and the commandment holy,
and just, and good" (Rom. 7:12). The Mosaic law was the specific
revelation of the moral law of God to Israel (Rom. 9:4). It was
therefore good because any manifestation of a good God must
necessarily also be good (James 1:17). The law, however, was not
given to be the instrument of salvation because no man was ca-
pable of keeping it (Gal. 3:21). Throughout, God intended to
stimulate within man a consciousness of sin and guilt whereby the
convicted sinner would turn to the gracious provision of God for
redemption.

1. Character of the law

Three observations are given. *First*, the law was "the handwrit-
ing of ordinances." The first word (cheirographon) is found in the
papyri and indicates a certificate of debt on which the signature of
the debtor was inscribed. Paul alluded to this custom when he

---

[10]The aorist participle ("having forgiven") gives action antecedent to the main
verb ("quickened").

voluntarily assumed the debt of Onesimus: "I Paul have written it with mine own hand, I will repay it." (Philem. 19). When the debt was canceled, a large "X" was placed over the document. In a similar vein, the ordinances of the Mosaic law written by God through Moses declare the debt of sinful man to God. He has come under its curse because he has not kept all of the laws all of the time (Gal. 3:10; James 2:10).

Second, the law was "against us" *(kath hēmōn)*. It offered no hope nor encouragement. It demanded judgment without mercy (Heb. 10:26–28). Homer A. Kent, Jr., likened it to "an unpaid bill turned over to a bill collector."[11]

Third, the law was "contrary to us." It was hostile. Carson explained: "The law of God not only stated our guilt, but cried out for the penalty due to such guilt."[12] The law was the prosecuting attorney, judge, jury, and executioner of the sinner.

2. Action of Christ

In His death and resurrection, Christ dealt with the law in three ways. *First*, He dealt with it by "blotting" it out *(exaleipsas)*. He erased it, wiped it off, rubbed it out (cf. Acts 3:19; Rev. 3:5). With a cry of triumph, Jesus exclaimed: "It is finished" (John 19:30). The payment was full and final.

Second, He "took it out of the way." The perfect tense of the verb *(ērken)* indicates the permanence of the removal. The believer has no fear that the penalty for a broken law will later be exacted from him. The verb also shows that the law cannot be the basis of sanctification. In order to create the church, Christ had to remove two barriers: sin (which separated the sinner from God) and the law (which formed a fence between Jew and Gentile). Jesus' death accomplished this double result:

> For he is our peace, who hath made both one, and hath broken down the middle wall of partition between us;
> Having abolished in his flesh the enmity, even the law of com-

---

[11] Homer A. Kent, Jr., *Treasures of Wisdom: Studies in Colossians and Philemon*, p. 88.

[12] Carson, *Epistles of Paul*, p. 69.

mandments contained in ordinances; for to make himself of twain one new man, so making peace (Eph. 2:14–15).

Third, He "nailed it to his cross." A superscription was placed on the cross by Pilate to show the crime for which Christ was crucified: "JESUS OF NAZARETH THE KING OF THE JEWS" (John 19:19).[13] In His atonement, however, Christ cancelled the debt of mankind to the law. His death covered all trespasses: past, present, and future.

E. Triumph over Powers (2:15)

The heretics incorrectly elevated the role of angels in creation and redemption. Paul demonstrated that the cross directly affected the genuine activity of angels. There is disagreement whether these angels are good or evil. If they are good, then the death of Christ ended the mediation of these angels in the giving of the law (Acts 7:53; Gal. 3:19; Heb. 2:2). If they are evil, then He triumphed over Satan and the fallen angels through His death and resurrection (Gen. 3:15). Since both concepts are true, it is difficult to determine which view is in mind here. The second position is the common choice of most evangelicals.

1. He spoiled them

At the cross, Christ "spoiled principalities and powers." These two areas of supernatural authority can refer to the entire angelic world, both good and bad, or to either one in particular (1:16; 2:10; Eph. 6:12). The verb "spoiled" (*apekdusamenos*) means "to put off away from." It often is translated as "put off" (2:11; 3:9). The metaphor refers to a person who strips off his clothes.

If these are evil angels, then Christ stripped from them their evil power. He bruised the head of Satan (Gen. 3:15) and destroyed this angelic ruler who had the power to keep men in the realm of death (Heb. 2:14). When Christ cast out demons during His earthly ministry, He gave this defense of His actions:

[13] The full writing, "This is Jesus of Nazareth, the King of the Jews," is gleaned from a study of all four Gospels (cf. Matt. 27:37; Mark 15:26; Luke 23:38).

> But if I with the finger of God cast out devils [demons], no doubt the kingdom of God is come upon you.
>
> When a strong man armed keepeth his palace, his goods are in peace:
>
> But when a stronger than he shall come upon him, and overcome him, he taketh from him all his armor wherein he trusted and divideth his spoils (Luke 11:20–22).

Satan is a defeated foe; nevertheless, he can still do terrible spiritual damage (I Peter 5:8). His ultimate doom in the lake of fire was secured at the cross (Matt. 25:41; Rev. 20:10).

2. He displayed them

Next, Christ "made a show of them openly." The verb (edeigmatisen) means "to display, publish, or proclaim." It was used of Joseph, who did not want "to make her [Mary] a publick example" (Matt. 1:19; same word). At the cross, Satan "the prince of the world was cast out" (John 12:31). The evil one was "as lightning fallen from heaven" (Luke 10:18). In His descent into and ascent out of Hades, Christ gained the keys of death and hell (Rev. 1:18). He proclaimed to the evil spirits in the prison of Tartarus that their multiple attempts to destroy the redemptive line from Adam to the promised Messiah had failed (I Peter 3:19; II Peter 2:4).

3. He triumphed over them

The imagery behind the verb "triumphing" (thriambeusas) is taken from the processions of ancient Roman emperors and generals who led the captives taken in battle and exposed them to the gaze of a cheering public. Believers are part of the victorious army, enjoying the triumphant march as they follow their spiritual king (II Cor. 2:14).

Questions for Discussion

1. What are the qualities of true humanity? How did Christ manifest these in His earthly existence? since the resurrection?

2. What is involved in positional completeness? How does this truth support the doctrine of eternal security?

3. In what ways do the cults use regulations to help their adherents gain perfection? How can cult members be rescued from this conformity?

4. In what ways do contemporary Christians identify outward rites with inner reality?

5. What are the various views of water baptism? spiritual baptism? How are those views different? How are they the same?

6. What part should the Mosaic law have in the life of the believer today? Are Christians basically legalistic?

7. In what ways can believers claim victory over Satan because of the cross? Why are so many living defeated lives?

The Contrast in Doctrine
Colossians 2:16—3:4

God gave Israel criteria by which she could determine whether a prophet was genuine or false (Deut. 18:15–22). Christ also set forth such guidelines (Matt. 7:15–20). John, a representative of the apostles, cautioned: "Beloved, believe not every spirit, but try the spirits whether they are of God: because many false prophets are gone out into the world" (I John 4:1).

In this section (2:16—3:4), Paul, too, challenges his readers to evaluate their beliefs. Using this theme he concludes the first half of the epistle and establishes the transition to the second half, which deals specifically with practical Christian experience (3:5—4:6). The logical connective "therefore" *(oun)* points back to the preceding verses where the apostle demonstrated that through His death and resurrection Christ fulfilled the obligations of the believer to the Mosaic law.

I. THE PRACTICE OF FALSE DOCTRINE (2:16–23)

Paul earlier warned against the Gnostic, deceitful philosophy which was humanistic, legalistic, and non-Christian (2:8). Now he refutes three specific areas of false practice within the heresy which threatened the church.

A. Legalism (2:16–17)

Many Jewish Christians continued to circumcise their children and to be zealous for the law (Acts 21:20–24). They recognized that Gentiles who had been saved out of paganism did not need to observe these practices (Acts 15:28–29; 21:25). The Gnostic Judaizers, however, tried to impose Mosaic legalism on the Colossians as the means to spiritual perfection. When that which was optional became mandatory, Paul had to act. He commanded the church to stop the procedure of judgment ("Let no man judge you"). The present tense of the imperative *(krinetō)* indicates that the heretics and their converts constantly had been criticizing the lack of legal conformity within the church. This issue was far more severe than differences of opinion within the areas of Christian liberty (Rom. 14:1–15; I Cor. 8:1–13).

1. Areas of legalism (2:16)

Five areas are listed. *First*, the phrase "in meat" *(en brōsei)* encompasses the entire area of eating. It denotes Jewish dietary regulations with their distinction between clean and unclean foods (Lev. 11; Acts 10:14). The Pharisees extended the restrictions by requiring people to bathe and to wash their hands before eating (Mark 7:1–23). Later, Paul warned against those who commanded others "to abstain from meats" (I Tim. 4:2). Since Christ's death and resurrection, all foods reflect divine provision and should be received with thanksgiving (Mark 7:18–23; Acts 10:15; I Cor. 10:25–26; I Tim. 4:3–5). It is plausible that the heretics might have taught that certain foods helped the mind to develop a spiritual sensitivity, whereas others prevented that.

Second, the area of "drink" *(posei)* probably included the prohibition of wine and strong drink. Levites and Nazarites observed this restriction (Lev. 10:9; Num. 6:3). Liquids could not be stored in unclean vessels (Lev. 11:34–36). Elsewhere, Paul commented that "the kingdom of God is not meat and drink; but righteousness, and peace, and joy in the Holy Spirit" (Rom. 14:17).

Third, the "holyday" was literally a "feast" *(heortēs)*. The three major feasts in the Jewish calendar were Passover, Pentecost, and Tabernacles (Exod. 23:14–18). At those times, all Jewish males were to worship God at Jerusalem through the sacrificial system. Even the Jewish apostle Paul desired to keep such a feast (Acts 18:21).

Fourth, the "new moon" marked the observance of the lunar

calendar (Num. 10:10; 28:11; I Sam. 20:18). It was a day of rest, worship, fellowship, and eating. Elsewhere, Paul lamented: "Ye observe days, and months, and times, and years" (Gal. 4:10).

Fifth, the "sabbath days" *(sabbatōn)* pointed to Saturday, the day of weekly rest in which Israel remembered the divine work of creation and her covenant relationship (Exod. 20:8–11; 31:12–18). The Christian, however, should remember the work of spiritual creation by gathering in the local church on Sunday, the day on which Christ rose from the dead (Acts 20:7; I Cor. 16:2).

2. Weakness of legalism (2:17)

The Mosaic law, with its moral and ceremonial regulations, was "a shadow of things to come." This is expressed elsewhere: "For the law having a shadow of good things to come, and not the very image of the things, can never with those sacrifices which they offered year by year continually make the comers thereunto perfect" (Heb. 10:1). A shadow does not exist in and of itself. It is caused by a material object or person. It has reality only in that it points to the substance which formed it.

In like fashion, the law was given to produce a sense of moral guilt and to drive the convicted sinner to put his faith in the gracious provision of God, namely, Christ (Gal. 3:24). The sacrificial calendar produced pictures or types of what Christ would accomplish in His death and resurrection (Heb. 9:13–14). He is the passover for the believer (I Cor. 5:7), the open veil into the very presence of God (Heb. 10:19–20).

In real life, one embraces the body, not the shadow. Christ becomes "the end of the law for righteousness to every one that believeth" (Rom. 10:4).

B. Angel Worship (2:18–19)

In this area, the apostle warned: "Let no man beguile you of your reward." These eight words actually translate three Greek terms *(medeis humas katabrabeuetō)*. This verb is related to two words: "prize" *(brabeion;* I Cor. 9:24; Phil. 3:14) and "umpire" *(brabeus)*. Paul used this second term later: "And let the peace of God rule [as umpire] in your hearts" (3:15). Because of the double relationship, the warning allows for two different interpretations. First, the believer could lose his reward at the judgment seat of Christ if he fails to maintain his doctrinal steadfastness (II John 8). Second, the believer should stop anyone from giving an official judgment against his lack of legalism (Rom. 14:12–13). Although both positions are biblically correct, the second seems to be more plausible in this context.

1. It promotes self (2:18–19a)

Four participial phrases describe the false teacher ("no man") who tried to force error on the Colossians.[1] *First,* he was marked by a "voluntary humility and worshipping of angels." The adjective "voluntary" is a participle *(thelōn)* which denotes the act of willing or choosing. This person decided to manifest humility *(tapeinophrosunēi;* cf. 2:23). Genuine humility, produced by the Spirit of God, is commendable (Acts 20:19; Eph. 4:2; Phil 2:3; Col. 3:12; I Peter 5:5); however, this heretic took delight in his humility.[2] It could have been either a false or a true self-abasement. If it was the former, he did it for external appearance; if it was the latter, he may have sincerely believed that he was unworthy to go directly to God. This premise would thus form the basis for his respect for the angels. The emphasis of this worship *(thrēskeia)* is on ceremonial rites and conformity. Although the false teacher's humility was impressive to others, it achieved erroneous results.

Second, the false teacher intruded into a forbidden area. The participle "intruding" *(embateuōn)*[3] was used "of an initiate in the mysteries who 'set foot in' and performed the rest of the rites."[4] The area of intrusion is debatable. He moved into either the realm of the invisible ("into those things which he hath not seen") or the domain of the visible ("those things which he hath seen").[5]

---

[1] They are all nominative singular participles, agreeing with the subject of the imperative *(mēdeis).*
[2] The RSV renders the phrase as, "insisting on self-abasement."
[3] Used only here in the New Testament.
[4] A. T. Robertson, *Word Pictures in the New Testament,* vol. 4, p. 497.
[5] The critical Greek text omits the negative.

The reason for the difference may lie in the supposition that the false teachers claimed to have special visions and revelations which they alone witnessed. In any case, they elevated extrabiblical content and based their authoritative teaching on what they personally had experienced.

Third, the false teacher was "vainly puffed up by his fleshly mind." He felt superior because of what he knew, what he could see, and what he could reason. Believers should grow in spiritual knowledge as they are taught by God through His Word, but a false biblical intellectualism is empty or vain *(eikē)*. The imagery behind "puffed up" *(phusioumenos)* is that of a pair of bellows *(phusa)* which are used to blow up or inflate *(phusioō)*. Such knowledge apart from love is self-destructive (I Cor. 4:6, 18; 8:1). His knowledge was produced by the sinful human flesh rather than by the Spirit of God.

Fourth, the false teacher did not elevate Christ, the head of the church ("not holding the Head"). The negative *(ou)* is very emphatic.[6] The present participle *(kratōn)* shows that he was continually not elevating the Savior. In fact, all four participles describe a constant pattern of belief and behavior. Although this false teacher had gained some preeminence in the church, he was actually unsaved. He personified the warning of Christ: "Beware of false prophets, which come to you in sheep's clothing, but inwardly they are ravening wolves" (Matt. 7:15).

2. It demotes Christ (2:19b)

The Holy Spirit came to glorify Christ (John 16:4). Paul gloried in the cross of the Savior (Gal. 6:14). In the church, Christ should have all the preeminence (1:18). The distinctive feature of all heretical sects within professing Christendom, however, is a total or partial denial of the divine-human person of Christ and His redemptive death and bodily resurrection.

The intellectual, legalistic teaching at Colosse likewise did not properly esteem Christ. In its worship of angels, it denied to Christ four areas of emphasis. *First*, He alone is "the Head" of the body, the church (1:18). There can be only one head, "from

[6]The normal negative for a participle is *mē*.

which" *(ex hou)* the body can receive life and direction.[7] The elevation of angels and a Gnostic caste system constitute many heads.

Second, Christ nourishes the body ("from which all the body by joints and bands having nourishment ministered"). This spiritual food and strength come from the Word of God as it is ministered by gifted teachers under the control of the Holy Spirit (Eph. 4:11–16; Phil. 1:19). The participle "having nourishment" *(epichorēgoumenon)* means "to furnish supplies for a musical chorus." In ancient times, a benefactor would pay for the singers and the dancers at a festival. In time the word came to mean "to provide generously." In medical terminology, it was used of the joints and ligaments which joined two bones together (Eph. 4:16). As a man nourishes and cherishes his physical body, so Christ ministers to His spiritual body, the church (Eph. 5:29).

Third, Christ unites the church. The participle "knit together" *(sumbibazomenon)* was used earlier in the epistle (2:2). The body is "compacted [same word] by that which every joint supplieth, according to the effectual working in the measure of every part" (Eph. 4:16). The joints and ligaments are the means of unity as well as the means of sustenance. In a similar manner, Christ came to build *one* church (Matt. 16:18; Eph. 4:4–6).

Fourth, Christ increases the church ("increaseth with the increase of God"). Christ, not man, is the builder. As believers elevate and love Christ, they will love each other. The result will be the "increase of the body unto the edifying of itself in love" (Eph. 4:16).

C. Asceticism (2:20–23)

Asceticism and legalism are partners in humanistic religion. Asceticism promotes self-denial, the deliberate refusal to have material comforts in order to develop spiritual sensitivity. It usually leads to fasting, celibacy, and the monastic life. It initially gives the impression of total dedication, but it actually is contrary to grace living and to the practice of a believer's position in Christ.

[7]The relative pronoun *(hou)* is masculine, agreeing with Christ, the understood appositive to the "head" (feminine noun).

THE CONTRAST IN DOCTRINE

1. Its ignorance (2:20)

The professing Christian who practices asceticism is ignorant of three basic facts. *First,* the believer has died positionally in Christ. Paul did not doubt the salvation experience of the Colossian believers; rather, he assumed it as the basis of his argument. This first class conditional clause can be translated: "If therefore ye died with Christ, and ye have . . . ."[8] It could even be rendered: "Since ye died with Christ." At conversion, the believing sinner was baptized in the Holy Spirit into Christ (I Cor. 12:13). The result is a positional, judicial identification with Christ in His actual death on the cross. The believer died "with Christ" *(sun tōi Christōi)* when He satisfied the righteous demands for a broken law. This fundamental truth must be known and appropriated in order to live a victorious life over sin (Rom. 6:1–10).

Second, the believer has thus been separated "from the rudiments of the world." Death brings separation and freedom from prior obligation (Rom 7:1–6). These legalistic regulations originate within the world of lost humanity and represent their attempt to gain favor before God (cf. 2:8; Gal. 4:3). They are "weak" in that they are powerless to provide redemption, and they are "beggarly" in that they cannot supply a spiritual inheritance (Gal. 4:9).

Third, the believer does not need to yield to legalism. The question supports that conclusion drawn from the assumed reality of the condition: ". . . why, as though living in the world, are ye subject to ordinances?" Believers are still in the world, but they are no longer of the world (John 15:19). They should use, not abuse, the world (I Cor. 7:31). They should resist human dogmas *(dogmatizesthe)* which stem from a wordly system of self-righteousness and which are brought into the church under the guise of submission and humility. These attempts to gain spirituality through outward conformity and physical deprivation are many.

2. Its description (2:21)

Legalists and ascetics always emphasize the negative. They assert that spirituality is measured by an absence of prescribed sins,

---

[8] It uses the conditional particle *ei* with the aorist indicative *apethanete*. It is the same type as that in 1:23.

rather than by the presence of positive virtues. Three examples of their prohibitions are given.[9] *First,* "touch not" *(mē hapsēi).* Since the third imperative also deals with the sense of touch, this command may stress sexual abstinence for those who are married and the prevention of marriage for those who were single. Paul did allow for temporary sexual abstinence within marriage for religious reasons and he encouraged the single life as exemplified in his own practice (I Cor. 7:1, 5, 7–8, 34). He wrote: "It is good for a man not to touch [same word] a woman" (I Cor. 7:1). These Pauline instructions could have easily been distorted by the heretics. Later, Paul advised Timothy to watch for apostates who prohibited marriage (I Tim. 4:3). The false teachers doubtless charged that physical marital privileges had to be forfeited in order to gain a sensitivity to the spiritual marriage of believers to Christ.

Second, "taste not" *(mēde geusēi).* This command encouraged fasting and a prescribed diet. Avoiding specific foods was deemed necessary for the preparation of visions and for promoting a desire for the food of the soul (cf. Dan. 10:2–3). Quite often, such asceticism leads to vegetarianism. Certain foods are looked upon as essential for the development of the mind and the elimination of bodily poisons. However, all foods, both meat and vegetables, can be eaten by the believer today if they are received with thanksgiving (I Tim. 4:3–5).

Third, "handle not" *(mēde thigēis).* A person must touch before he can taste. This legalistic command prohibited even the mere handling of a forbidden food. It is reminiscent of Eve's response to the inquiry of Satan: "But of the fruit of the tree which is in the midst of the garden, God hath said, Ye shall not eat of it, neither shall ye touch it, lest ye die" (Gen. 3:3). The legalist is afraid of even an occasional contact with an item whose usage is forbidden to him.

3. *Its weakness (2:22–23)*

Legalists look on their asceticism as a spiritual strength, but ac-

---

[9]The stress in all three is upon the prevention of action. All are aorist subjunctives and convey this idea: "Do not begin to do it."

tually it is a weakness and an obstacle to true Christian living. Four aspects of its weakness are discussed here. *First,* it permits the material to dominate the spiritual. Kent observed: "How can such things have authority over man if he can destroy them by using them up?"[10] The forbidden things are those "which all are to perish with the using." God created sex, food, drink, and the desires to have them. Sin occurs through their abuse, not by their nonuse. A believer must not permit these temporal drives to control his life; he must control them through proper usage and the recognition of Christ's sovereignty over his life (I Cor. 6:12–13). He must not view certain foods, which are morally neutral, as either satanic or divine. Paul wrote concerning meat which had been offered to an idol: "But meat commendeth us not to God: for neither, if we eat, are we the better; neither, if we eat not, are we the worse" (I Cor. 8:8).

Second, asceticism originates with man ("after the commandments and doctrines of men"). Christ never imposed asceticism on the church. In fact, He taught that dietary restrictions push aside the divine commandment in favor of a human tradition (Mark 7:6–9). He further elucidated: "There is nothing from without a man, that entering into him can defile him: but the things which come out of him, those are they that defile the man" (Mark 7:15). The distinction between "commandments" *(entalmata)* and "doctrines" *(didaskalias)* is subtle because both words describe the same ascetic prohibition.[11] By one interpretation, the former may refer to the actual command and the latter to its explanation and application. According to another interpretation, the former might point to that which is written and the latter to that which is spoken. In this second view, the written commandments could include the regulations within the Mosaic law.

Third, asceticism is hypocritical. It has an impressive reputation. The world is usually awed by ascetics. The commandments and teachings of legalism "have indeed a show of wisdom." The term "show" *(logon)* normally translates as "word" and connotes

---

[10] Homer A. Kent, Jr., *Treasures of Wisdom; Studies in Colossians and Philemon,* p. 100.

[11] The Granville Sharp rule is seen here: *kata ta entalmata kai didaskalias.*

the idea of a verbal report or transmitted rumor. To the adherents, the regulations are rational and logical. This false religious intellectualism becomes even more deceptive because it operates in the domain of three aspects. First, it functions "in will worship" *(ethelothrēskeiai)*. This self-imposed restriction manifested a choice to display the rigor of devotion in a unique way. It originated within the human will and not from divine revelation (cf. 2:18). Second, it is marked by "humility" (cf. 2:18; same word). Third, it punishes the body ("neglecting of the body"). The verbal noun *(apheidiāi)* comes from a term which means "to spare" *(pheidomai)*; thus, the word connotes an unsparing severity. This manifests itself in the denial of sleep, self-imposed beatings, and fasting.

Fourth, asceticism cannot overcome the power of the sin nature ("not in any honour to the satisfying of the flesh"). The word "honour" *(timēi)* conveys the idea of value or price; thus, legalism has no value in the fulfillment of victory over the flesh. In fact, Carson argued: "Asceticism does not do honor to the body, but only promotes the indulgence of the flesh."[12] Asceticism actually becomes an enemy to the Spirit-controlled life. The more legalistic one becomes, the more powerful the sin nature is. Regulations "lack any value in restraining sensual indulgence" (2:23, NIV). The cure for sins of the flesh is submission to the Holy Spirit, not conformity to a list of laws.

II. THE PRINCIPLES OF TRUE DOCTRINE (3:1–4)

The transition between the false and the true doctrines is made in two ways. First, the logical connective "then" *(oun)* joins them. Second, there is a parallelism in the identification of the believer with Christ in His death and then in His resurrection (2:20; cf. 3:1). A genuine teacher not only informs his people about what is wrong, but he also guides them into what is right. The two major divisions of this section are developed around two commands: "seek" and "set."

---

[12] Herbert M. Carson, *The Epistles of Paul to the Colossians and to Philemon*, p. 79.

THE CONTRAST IN DOCTRINE

A. Seek Heavenly Things (3:1)

The present imperative stresses constant, daily seeking (*zēte-ite*). It can be translated: "Keep on seeking." Christian perfection is a goal which demands diligent pursuit. The horizon of spiritual attainment grows broader as the believer advances higher and further into the will of God.

1. Its basis

Paul assumed that the Colossians positionally were identified with Christ. The first class conditional clause can be rendered: "If ye then be risen with Christ, and you have been."[13] Through positional identification, all believers have died with Christ, have been buried with Him, have been raised with Him, and have been seated with Him in the presence of God (2:12, 20; 3:1; Rom. 6:3–5; Eph. 2:5–6). In the redemptive program, God always sees the converted sinner is in Christ; therefore, whatever Christ has done, is also done in the believer. This divine reckoning becomes real in the life of the sinner at the time of his regeneration, but he must appropriate this truth daily in order to live the normal, victorious Christian life.

2. Its object

This object is stated in two ways. First, a believer should seek "those things which are above." If he is not heavenly-minded, he will never be any earthly good. The "above things" (*ta anō*) are in contrast to the "below things," the legalistic, ascetic practices of the heretics. The proper objects of seeking include the presence of God, the holy city, the total possession of "all spiritual blessings in heavenly places in Christ" (Eph. 1:3). The process of seeking incorporates the revealed will of God for one's life, the essence of all that one should become in Christ. Elsewhere, Paul testified: "I press toward the mark for the prize of the high [*anō*] calling of God in Christ Jesus" (Phil. 3:14).

Second, believers should seek "where Christ sitteth on the right hand of God." They should seek Him, as the Magi did.

---

[13] Again, it could be translated: "Since you were raised with Christ."

They should seek Him in whom all of the truths of their position-al acceptance are found. That Christ was exalted, and constantly sits at God's right hand, shows that His redemptive work was fin-ished (Phil. 2:9; Heb. 1:3; 10:12).[14]

B. Think Heavenly Things (3:2–4)

The second imperative ("Set your affection") deals more with the mind than with the feelings. It literally translates, "keep on thinking" (*phroneite*).[15] The verb form was changed to the Eng-lish noun "mind" in these complementary passages: "likeminded" and "one mind" (Phil. 2:2) and "this mind" (Phil. 2:5). Whereas the first command ("seek") deals with the will and active pursuit, the second charge refers to the mind. This is comparable to a marathon runner who is thinking about the race as he attempts to cross the finish line first. The seeking and the thinking should occur simultaneously.

1. Its object (3:2)

This object is stated both positively and negatively. *First*, the believer should think "on things above" (*ta anō*). This phrase is greatly emphasized because it occurs both first in the sentence and before the verb. It points out spiritual realities which have their source in God. It does not refer to future events exclusively, such as life after death and the eternal state, although it includes those truths as they affect present behavior (I John 3:1–3).

Second, the believer should not think "on things on the earth." In the context, the primary interpretation and application are to the intellectual, legalistic, and ascetic regulations imposed by the Gnostic, Judaistic teachers. In a secondary fashion, they include all earthly involvements which retard genuine spiritual develop-ment. The yielded Christian makes no distinction between the sa-cred and the secular; to him, everything must be done for the glory of God (3:17; I Cor. 10:31). This includes personal, family, and social responsibilities (3:5—4:6). However, he must differen-

---

[14]This emphasis is indicated by the periphrastic usage of the present parti-ciple: *estin . . . kathēmenos*.

[15]Present active imperative.

tiate between that which is beneficial and that which is detrimental to his spiritual health (Phil. 1:9–10).

2. Its reason (3:3–4)

Five reasons are given for heavenly thinking.[16] *First*, the believer died in Christ ("ye are dead"). The verb (*apethanete*; cf. 2:20) looks back to the cross when the child of God died positionally in Christ. In the actual life, this occurred at the moment of salvation. This reality has separated the believer forever from any obligation to a worldly legalism. As a wife is loosed from marital law through the death of her husband, so a believer becomes "dead to the law by the body of Christ" (Rom. 7:4).

Second, the life of the believer "is hid with Christ in God." The perfect verb (*kekruptai*) stresses the resultant state of safety and secrecy which a believer presently possesses because he trusted Christ as Savior in the past. It is hidden to the lost because no unsaved person can understand the mystical identification of the believer in Christ. This truth is part of the revealed mystery (1:26–27). It fulfills the prediction of Christ: "At that day ye shall know that I am in my Father, and ye in me, and I in you" (John 14:20).

Third, Christ is the very life of the believer ("our life"). He is the bread from heaven which men must eat by faith (John 6:51). As the living vine, He lives out His life through the branches, the believers (John 15:1–5).

Fourth, Christ "shall appear" (*phanerōthēi*) from heaven. From that standpoint, it becomes logical for a believer to look up rather than to look down or around. The temporal "when" (*hotan*) is better translated as "whenever." The fact of Christ's return is certain, but its time is indefinite. Since the believer does not know when that great event will occur, he must be constantly watching.

Fifth, the glorification of the believer will occur in heaven. The believer died and rose with Christ; in that future day, he will appear with Christ ("with Him"). The verb (*phanerōthēsesthe*) means "to make visible what is invisible."[17] When Christ returns,

---

[16] The explanatory connective "for" (*gar*) introduces this section.

[17] Kent, *Treasures of Wisdom*, p. 110.

the real position of the believer, which has been hidden to the world, will be made known. "Glory" comes from the total transformation of the person as evidenced in the immortal, incorruptible body, not from outward conformity to earthly laws. With such heavenly vision, Paul could boast: "For I reckon that the sufferings of this present time are not worthy to be compared with the glory which shall be revealed in us" (Rom. 8:18).

Questions for Discussion

1. In what erroneous ways do believers judge other believers today? What legalistic practices have replaced conformity to the Mosaic law?

2. What types of Christ can be seen in the Jewish sacrificial system? How did Christ fulfill those types in His life and ministry?

3. In what ways (e.g., moral or doctrinal) can believers lose their rewards? How can they prevent this from happening?

4. What church practices fail to exalt Christ as the head of the church? What church practices are acceptable? Why?

5. How can a person distinguish between true and false humility? How does humility relate to spiritual boldness and aggressiveness?

6. How can a believer help himself to seek and to think heavenly things? What earthly things can hold him back?

7. What positional truths will become realities at the return of Christ? How should they affect present behavior?

9

The Change in Behavior
Colossians 3:5–17

A change in position must be manifested in a change of practice. Paul demonstrated clearly that the identification of the believer with Christ in His death, resurrection, and ascension had set him free from the pressures of legalism, asceticism, and false intellectualism. This new standing should result in heavenly seeking and thinking.

The transition to the new section can be seen in the logical connective "therefore" *(oun)*. The general principles of a pursuit for holiness are now spelled out in specific patterns of behavior. Proper Christian living is both negative (3:5–11) and positive (3:12–17). The former involves the elimination of the past sins of the old unsaved life and the latter describes the development of a righteous character within the new life.

I. THE OLD LIFE (3:5–11)

The believer must willingly and actively overcome the desires of the sin nature within him. Paul appealed for this type of obedience by the usage of three direct imperatives (3:5, 8, 9). The first deals with sexual sins committed with the cooperation of others (3:5–7), the second with personal attitudes (3:8), and the third with sin aimed at fellow believers (3:9–11).

A. Mortify (3:5–7)

The believer has died in Christ, but he is still alive in the world (2:20); therefore, he must actuate his position. He must "mortify" *(nekrōsate)* the old life. The imperative stresses determination and decisive action.[1] It means "to render as dead, to regard as impotent." Abraham did not look on the impotence or deadness of his aged body as an obstacle to the birth of a promised son (Rom. 4:19; Heb. 11:12). Elsewhere, Paul charged: "Likewise reckon ye also yourselves to be dead [same word] unto sin" (Rom. 6:11). Thus, the believer cannot eradicate the sin nature, but he can treat it as a morally impotent force in his life.

The object of spiritual mortification is the "members which are upon the earth." The will of the believer must respond negatively to the impulses of the sin nature to use the physical parts of the human body for illicit purposes (I Cor. 6:13–20).

1. List of sins

Five sins are mentioned. "Fornication" *(porneian)* is a general word for sexual immorality, both within and without the marital union.[2] It is based upon two verbs *(peraō* and *pernēmi)* which convey the idea of selling bodies, both male and female, for lustful purposes. It is specifically used of the prostitute (James 2:25; Rev. 17:1, 5).

"Uncleanness" *(akatharsian)* is moral impurity in all forms. It is marked by a filthy mind, full of sensually suggestive thoughts and humor (Eph. 5:3–4). It reads illicit sex even into the most wholesome situations. Marked by perverted fantasies, it is expressed today through pornographic literature and movies. Caused by the lusts of the heart, it leads to the dishonor of bodies (Rom. 1:24).

"Inordinate affection" *(pathos)* is erotic love, depraved passion, uncontrollable desire. It desires to use another for one's own selfish, sensual gratification. It is both heterosexual and homosexual in character (Rom. 1:26; I Thess. 4:5).

"Evil concupiscence" *(epithumian kakēn)* is literally a "wicked desire." The physical desires created within the human anatomy and personality are divinely given and intrinsically good, but they

---

[1] Aorist active imperative. It could be ingressive ("Begin to mortify") or constative ("Throughout your life, mortify").

[2] The term *pornography* is based upon this Greek word.

become evil when they are motivated by the sin nature and are executed for evil ends.

A specific type of "covetousness" *(tēn pleonexian)* manifests the essence of "idolatry."[3] The word means "to have more." When Israel worshiped idols, she committed spiritual adultery because she wanted more than what her spiritual husband, God, gave her. In like manner, a person who commits adultery commits spiritual idolatry. In both cases, the exclusiveness of love and commitment to one is forsaken for another. Paul warned against defrauding [same word] the partner in the marriage relationship (I Thess. 4:6).

2. Judgment for sins (3:6)

Four truths can be gleaned. *First,* men bring divine judgment on themselves. The causal phrase, "for which things' sake," is a prepositional phrase *(di' ha)* which gives the reason why they should be judged. Men will reap that which they have sown (Gal. 6:7).

Second, the holiness of God and His righteous displeasure over sin are expressed in the phrase "the wrath of God." With God, such anger is judicial rather than temperamental; it is balanced within His holy being by mercy, compassion, and love. Habakkuk knew that God could not condone sin when he made this confession: "O Lord, thou hast ordained them for judgment; and, O mighty God, thou hast established them for correction. Thou art of purer eyes than to behold evil, and canst not look on iniquity" (Hab. 1:12–13). When God sees sin in action, He is repulsed by it and is constrained to judge it. He cannot be indifferent nor eternally long-suffering.

Third, the divine wrath "cometh" *(erchetai,* "is coming").[4] The wrath of God presently abides on all who have not trusted Christ (John 3:36); thus, they can be designated as "the children of wrath" (Eph. 2:3). Unless they are saved, this judicial wrath will be transformed into the actual wrath of God. It is just as certain

---

[3]Note the usage of the Greek article with the noun and the presence of the qualitative relative pronoun "which" *(hētis).*

[4]It is a futuristic present.

and imminent as the return of Christ or physical death. The physical expression of divine wrath will occur during the great tribulation (Rev. 6:17), and its eternal manifestation in the lake of fire.

Fourth, only the "children of disobedience" will experience this divine wrath. Literally, they are the "sons" *(huious)* of disobedience.[5] Christ delivered the believer from all involvement in the divine wrath (I Thess. 1:10; 5:9).

3. Life in sins (3:7)

Two statements about the past life of believers are given. *First*, they once "walked" with those who had practiced such sins. The verb *(periepatēsate)* characterizes the entirety of their unsaved life (cf. 2:6).[6] Elsewhere Paul wrote: "Wherein in time past ye walked according to the course of this world, according to the prince of the power of the air, the spirit that now worketh in the children of disobedience" (Eph. 2:2). The prepositional phrase ("in the which") should be translated "among whom" *(en hois)*. The reference is to the people, rather than to the sins themselves.[7]

Second, believers also "lived in them." The imperfect verb *(ezēte)* stresses the daily continuity of their sinful practice when they used to live in the world of immoral men and deeds. It usually is translated: "You were living."

B. Put Off (3:8)

The transition to the second command can be seen in the contrast between the past and the present: "some time" *(pote)* and "now" *(nuni)*. It is further strengthened by the connective "also." The believer must refrain from these specific actions, but sinful attitudes must likewise be put off.

---

[5] The critical Greek text omits the final words of the verb: "on the children of disobedience." These words are found in Ephesians 5:6.

[6] It is a constative aorist.

[7] The relative pronoun is masculine, agreeing with its antecedent "sons." The sins are described in the neuter gender *(ha;* 3:6).

THE CHANGE IN BEHAVIOR

1. The command

The imagery behind the imperative is that of clothing. Before new garments of righteousness can be put on, the old rags of sin must be discarded. The verb, "put off," calls for decisive, immediate resolution.[8] The presence of the personal pronoun "ye" *(humeis)* reinforces the sense of urgency and responsibility. Just as a runner must lay aside (same word) every weight to run a successful race (Heb. 12:1), so a believer must put off the garments of sin in order to live a beautiful Christian life.

2. The sins

Five sins are listed as examples, although the command would definitely include all immoral attitudes ("all these"). "Anger" *(orgēn)* is the same word used for the wrath of God (3:6). Anger, in itself, is a proper emotion if it is controlled by the Holy Spirit and is exercised for holy reasons (Eph. 4:26). In the unsaved man and in the carnal believer, it is the inward attitude of the sinful flesh; thus it is innately wrong.

"Wrath" *(thumon)* is closely associated with anger. In fact, it is white-hot anger. It is uncontrolled rage expressed through outbursts of temper. Carson claimed that "anger speaks of the settled attitude, while wrath is the passionate outburst."[9] Anger is kept in, whereas wrath is let out.

"Malice"*(kakian)* is a general term for moral badness. It envelops personal animosity and malicious gossip. It emphasizes the principle of sin, whereas "wickedness" *(ponēria)* points out the practice of sin (I Cor. 5:8). One who acts with malice does wrong; one who acts with wickedness does wrong with pleasure (Rom. 1:18, 32).

"Blasphemy" can be directed toward both God and man. It comes from two words *(phēmi* and *blaptō)* which mean, respectively, to speak and to injure someone. It includes both abusive words and slander (James 3:9–10).

[8] Aorist middle imperative.

[9] Herbert M. Carson, *The Epistles of Paul to the Colossians and to Philemon*, p. 83.

"Filthy communication" *(aischrologian)* denotes disgraceful speech. Such words should produce shame for both the speaker and the listener. It is low, obscene, dirty talk. It is full of swearing and sexual innuendo (Eph. 5:4).

Such sins grieve the Holy Spirit and should be put away immediately (Eph. 4:30–31).

C. Lie Not (3:9–11)

The first two commands stressed a crisis decision, a determined resolution to put away the sinful practices of the past. The present imperative ("Lie not") points out daily interpersonal relationships within the church. It denotes two basic ideas: Stop lying if you have been doing it; and continually do not lie to one another. To lie is to tell a deliberate untruth, to create a wrong impression by revealing a partial truth, and to distort the facts by exaggeration. Elsewhere Paul wrote: "Wherefore putting away lying, speak every man truth with his neighbor: for we are members one of another" (Eph. 4:25). Lying must be replaced by the telling of truth before complete spiritual victory can be attained. The reason for this verbal transformation is the fact that believers are brothers and members of the body of Christ, the true church.

1. Part of the old life (3:9)

The opening six words ("seeing that ye have put off") are the translation of one Greek aorist participle which explains why a believer should stop lying *(apekdusamenoi)*. At conversion, the believing sinner positionally put off his old life; he passed from death to life, from being in Adam to being in Christ (John 5:24; Rom. 5:12–21). In his daily life, however, he must appropriate his spiritual identification with Christ and put off the actual practice of sin.

The past unsaved life is described as "the old man with his deeds." This phrase includes both the position and the practice of sin. When a person is genuinely saved, he desires to be delivered not only from the penalty of his lost position before God, but also from the power of the sin nature which causes him to practice sin. Jesus' death and resurrection provide this double aspect of salvation.

THE CHANGE IN BEHAVIOR

2. Contrary to the new life (3:10-11)

At regeneration, the believer not only put off the old position, but he also "put on" a new standing before God.[10] Or, in terms of the metaphor about clothing, he did not put the new over the old. A believer has only one position before God, although he has two natures: the old sin nature, and the new nature centered in the indwelling life of God. The new position guarantees heaven, and submission to the new nature brings spiritual victory (Gal. 5:16).

The new life is described in two ways. *First*, it has *positional newness* (3:10). It is "new" *(neon)* in contrast to that which is "old" *(palaion)*. It is not the old made new or the old reformed. The new has no connection whatsoever with the old. In the life of the person, the new life never existed until regeneration occurred.

In a literal translation, this life "is being renewed" *(anakainoumenon)*.[11] This participle denotes the process of progressive sanctification whereby the Holy Spirit is transforming the believer into Christ-likeness (Rom. 12:2; II Cor. 3:18; 4:16; Titus 3:5). The believer does not renew himself, but the Spirit works within him daily.

The goal of renewal is "knowledge" *(eis epignōsin)*. It indicates a full, comprehensive, personal knowledge. Paul wanted to know Christ in a deeper way (Phil. 3:10); thus, to know Him is to become like Him.

The standard of renewal is "after the image of him that created him." God created man in His own image (Gen. 1:26, 28). Man was originally constituted in knowledge, righteousness, and true holiness (Eph. 4:24). Through the first sin committed in the primeval garden, man lost the moral expression of that innate image, although he still retained the image itself (Gen. 9:6; James 3:9). Through regeneration and sanctification, the moral expression can gradually be restored to the life. Since Christ is *the* image of God (1:15), the standard of spiritual excellence is Christ Himself.

Second, the new life has *positional oneness* (3:11). The adverb

---

[10] Both participles are aorist, pointing out a completed action in the past.
[11] Present passive participle.

137

"where" refers to the new man, the spiritual position of every believer regardless of one's race, religion, culture, or social status. Elsewhere, Paul wrote: "There is neither Jew nor Greek, there is neither bond nor free, there is neither male nor female; for ye are all one in Christ Jesus" (Gal. 3:28). Christ is everything to the child of God, and He abides in every Christian. The first usage of "all" *(ta panta)* is neuter and looks at all the spiritual riches which a believer possesses in Christ (Eph. 1:3–14). He provides salvation; thus there is no need for angelic mediation (1:14–23). He provides satisfaction; thus there is no need for philosophy (1:26—2:8). He provides sanctification; thus there is no need for legalism and asceticism (2:9—3:17). The second usage of "all" *(pasi)* is masculine and points to the various classes of mankind just mentioned in the verse.

Four divisions of humanity are given here, although there are others (e.g., sex: male and female). *Race* is indicated by the couplet "Greek nor Jew." All non-Jews, including those of both Greek and Roman nationality, are classified as "Greek." *Religion* is seen in the contrast "circumcision nor uncircumcision." The former embraces Judaism with its pure Jewish adherents and Gentile proselytes; the latter points to the pagan world (Rom. 2:25–29; I Cor. 7:18–19). *Culture* is involved in the two terms "Barbarian, Scythian." The first refers to those who were ignorant of the culture and language of the Greeks and Romans in that day (Rom. 1:14). The Scythian was the lowest type of barbarian, a very crude and rough person, such as the nomads who roamed the areas around the Black and Caspian seas. *Social status* is revealed in the words "bond nor free." The Roman world of the first century was almost equally divided between slaves and freemen. In the church at Colosse, this distinction was very evident in the relationship between Onesimus and Philemon.

In actual life, these classifications remain, but in the church and in Christ, they are erased. There is no spiritual advantage or disadvantage in any of them (Gal. 6:15).

II. THE NEW LIFE (3:12–17)

The new life has already been introduced as "Christ" and "the new man" (3:4, 10). In this section, Paul set forth the new patterns of behavior that should manifest the new position. They are seen in a series of imperatives.

A. The Expression of the New Life (3:12–14)

The command ("put on") calls for a firm determination to practice what had already been done positionally (3:10).[12] It continues the imagery of clothing—the removal of the old and the replacement with the new.

1. Description of believers (3:12a)

Three descriptions are given. *First*, believers are "the elect of God." God sovereignly chose each one of them in Christ "before the foundation of the world that [they] should be holy and without blame before him in love" (Eph. 1:4). As the elect, they believed in Christ when they were convicted by the Holy Spirit and drawn to the Son by the Father (John 6:44; 16:7–11; Titus 1:1). As the justified elect, they can never be condemned spiritually (Rom. 8:33).

Second, believers are "holy" *(hagioi)*. The same word was used earlier of them and translated as "saints" (1:2). They had been permanently set apart from the world unto God for His unique possession.

Third, believers are "beloved" *(ēgapēmenoi)*. This verbal adjective indicates that God had fixed His love on them both at the cross and at their conversion and that they would remain the eternal objects of His love (Rom. 8:38–39).[13]

2. List of virtues (3:12b–14)

Eight virtues are delineated within four general categories. The first two show the believer's treatment of others; the next two, his estimation of himself; the next three, his reaction to ill treatment; and the final one, the all-pervasive principle of true discipleship.

The expression "bowels of mercies" *(splagchna oiktirmōn)* literally refers to the internal organs (especially the heart, liver, lungs and stomach); it implies softness and vulnerability. Thus, by ex-

---

[12] Aorist middle imperative.

[13] It is a perfect passive participle.

tension, the phrase denotes deep feelings of concern for the needs of others. God is merciful (Lam. 3:22); Christ manifested compassion when He performed miracles, and believers should become emotionally involved with others.

"Kindness" *(chrēstotēta)* is grace in action. It is a sweetness of disposition, a desire for the good of others. Translated as "gentleness," it is part of the fruit of the Spirit (Gal. 5:22). God manifests such acts of kindness toward sinners (Rom. 2:4; Eph. 2:7; Titus 3:4).

The phrase "humbleness of mind" translates one term *(tapeinophrosunēn)*. This positive quality causes a person to see himself as the object of divine grace. He recognizes that he has no right to assert himself. This proper attitude before God can be seen in his service toward others (Phil. 2:3). It manifests the mind of Christ (Phil. 2:5). It is the genuine expression of humility in contrast to the false, deceitful, self-imposed humility of the heretics (2:18, 23).

"Meekness" *(praiotēta)* is marked by courtesy and a spirit of quiet submission. It is not psychological timidity and weakness; rather, it is power under control. An ox within a yoke is meek, able to be turned in any direction by the will of its master. Meekness is the opposite of insubordination. Moses, Christ, and Paul were all meek (Num. 12:3; Matt. 11:29; I Cor. 4:21).

"Longsuffering" is literally "wrath that is put far away" *(makrothumia)*. One work of the flesh manifests a wrath that is near and inside (3:8; Gal. 5:20), but the Spirit-controlled believer puts distance between himself and this enemy (Gal. 5:22). It enables a Christian to put up with people who try his patience (II Cor. 6:6). He does not have a quick temper.

"Forbearing one another" means a person tolerates others when they irritate him. Forbearance has "an element of leniency, a willingness to suspend a rightful demand out of consideration for the plight or weakness of a fellow believer."[14] It seeks redemptive ends (Rom. 2:4; 3:25).

"Forgiving one another" is the climax of these other virtues. Its *meaning* is the gracious removal of sin and the gracious treatment

---

[14] Everett F. Harrison, *Colossians: Christ All-sufficient,* p. 89.

THE CHANGE IN BEHAVIOR

of the sinner who is unworthy to receive it. The verb *(charizome-noi)* is based on the Greek term for "grace" *(charis)*. Its *scope* is "one another." The change in Greek pronouns in this verse from *allēlōn* to *heautois* probably indicates a change from the general world of mankind to interpersonal relationships within the family of God. Its *need* is contained in the conditional clause ("if any man have a quarrel against any"). The term "quarrel" *(momphēn)* comes from the verb "to blame" *(memphomai)*; thus, it means a blameworthy cause, a matter for complaint. Its *standard* is divine forgiveness: "even as Christ forgave you, so also do ye." Vertical forgiveness should result in horizontal forgiveness. If Christ has forgiven believers of so much, then they should forgive each other of so little. His forgiveness is for time and eternity; ours is only for time. His embraced both the quality and the quantity of sins. There is no sin which He has not graciously remitted.

"Charity" *(agapēn;* usually translated as "love") holds all of the other virtues in place. The imagery is that of the oriental girdle which is placed "above" or "upon" *(epi)* all the other pieces of clothing. Thus, love is the girdle that holds the other spiritual qualities, figuratively described as clothing for the new man, in place. The phrase, "all these things," refers to the other spiritual virtues.

This love is distinctively Christian. It literally reads "the love" *(tēn agapēn)*. It is that type of love which has its source in God and which is divinely implanted within the child of God (I John 3:14; 4:8).

This love is the "bond of perfectness." As the "bond" *(sundes-mos)*, it is that which binds together practical righteousness. Earlier, Paul stated that he wanted the Colossians to be knit together in love (2:2). The "perfectness" is the goal toward which the apostle worked in his ministry (1:28). No believer has achieved spiritual maturity until all of his works of holiness are thoroughly encompassed by love. Without love, the good deeds are nothing (I Cor. 13).

B. The Controls of the New Life (3:15–17)

The practical application of the new position is further introduced in a series of four imperatives. They form the guidelines for the new life.

1. Peace (3:15a)

Three qualities of this peace are expressed. *First*, it is divine peace ("the peace of God").[15] Its character stems from its source, the Triune God: the Father (Phil. 4:7), the Son (John 14:27), and the Holy Spirit (Gal. 5:22). In the midst of circumstances which ordinarily cause anxiety, it protects the hearts and minds of believers; in that sense, it surpasses all human understanding (Phil. 4:7). It is that inner calmness of emotions and thoughts which rests on the assurance that God is too good to be unkind and too wise to make mistakes. It must be contrasted with the "peace with God" which is the result of a justified position (Rom. 5:1).

Second, it is a ruling peace ("rule in your hearts"). The verb (*brabeuetō*) means "to act as an umpire." Divine peace should constantly regulate all activities of the believer.[16] Peace should always overrule dissension. The heretics tried to usurp that authority by rendering a spiritual judgment against the church (2:18; *katabrabeuetō*). The domain of rule is the inner man ("hearts").

Third, it is a peace of unity. The prepositional phrase ("to which") refers back to the divine peace.[17] All believers were divinely "called in one body" to a position of peace before God and to a practice of peace within the true church. Peace and unity go together; one cannot exist without the other. Christ, the very peace of each believer, has made "in himself of twain one new man, so making peace" (Eph. 2:14–15).

2. Thanksgiving (3:15b)

The command literally reads: "And thankful continually become" (*kai eucharistoi ginesthe*). Paul earlier prayed that gratitude might mark the Colossians' lives (1:12). A thankful person acknowledges the working of the sovereign will of God in his life and circumstances (I Thess. 5:18). He should become thankful for

---

[15]The critical Greek text has "the peace of Christ."

[16]Indicated by the present active imperative.

[17]The relative pronoun (*hēn*) is in the feminine gender, agreeing with its antecedent (*eirēnē*).

the very being of God, salvation, life itself, family, and his fellow believers within the church.

3. Word of Christ (3:16)

The command has three key features. *First,* the "word of Christ" may refer to the word which Christ spoke on earth and which He revealed directly to the apostles (John 14:26; 15:7); in this sense, it is synonymous to "the word of the Lord" (I Thess. 1:8; 4:15; II Thess. 3:1).[18] It may, however, point out the Scripture which directly presents Him and His redemptive work.

Second, the imperative "dwell" *(enoiketō)* literally means "to be at home in." It is one thing for the believer to be in the Word; it is another for the Word to have free access to all parts of his life.

Third, the Word must dwell "richly" in order to be totally effective. It must be highly prized and appreciated. Harrison added that "it has to be cordially received, mixed with faith, appropriated in its fullness, and translated into action."[19] A believer must recognize that he is a spiritual pauper apart from it.

The consequences of the rich indwelling of the Word are indicated in the three participles: "teaching," "admonishing," and "singing." *First,* the believer will teach others "in all wisdom."[20] This wisdom is centered in Christ (2:3). Teaching emphasizes the positive instruction of truth.

Second, believers will admonish one another. The essence of admonition is warning and corrective function. The two ministries are to be conducted by three means. "Psalms" are the Old Testament Psalms sung to a musical accompaniment. Believers compose "hymns," which consist of praises to the glory of God. Some of these hymns have probably been incorporated into the inscripturated text (cf. I Tim. 1:15; 4:9). "Spiritual songs" embrace all other forms of biblical truth which promote an emotional and lyrical response within the child of God.

---

[18]This is the only place in the New Testament where the phrase "the word of Christ" occurs.

[19]Harrison, *Christ All-sufficient,* p. 91.

[20]The prepositional phrase, "in all wisdom," can go grammatically with either the imperative or the participle.

Third, believers will be "singing." Their songs will manifest thanks for the grace of God which has been given to them (I Cor. 10:30). They must express verbally what is a reality in their hearts. Song cannot be cold, lifeless, or without meaning. Since it originates in the heart, that removes technical artistry as a requirement for this ministry of edification. It must be done "to the Lord," not to entertain or to impress men.

4. Glory of God

Three features are involved in this command. *First,* the scope of activity is inclusive ("and whatsoever ye do in word or deed"). This statement refers to both what the believer says and what he does.

Second, activities should be done under the complete authority and approval of Jesus Christ ("do all in the name of the Lord Jesus"). He is the head of the church today and its ultimate judge. The "name" of Christ stands for all that He is and all that He has done. The Christian therefore should act in total conformity to his living Lord, as "those who bear His name."[21]

Third, a believer should always be thankful that God is his Father and that he has the unique privilege and responsibility to live for Him. He must constantly acknowledge that, as a sinner, he does not deserve to have anything in either this life or the next.

Questions for Discussion

1. Why do some believers commit condemned sins such as fornication? How can these sins be prevented?

2. Are some sins worse than others? Defend your answer.

3. How do Christians lie to one another? Is this the most common sin within the church?

4. What causes dissension and denominationalism? How can spiritual unity be achieved when so many differences exist today?

5. Is there a feeling of superiority within the church today? Relate your answer to education, finances, and race.

[21] Carson, *Epistles of Paul,* p. 91.

6. In what ways can Christians irritate each other? How should forbearance and forgiveness be manifested?

7. How do we give glory to God in our business life? family life? social life?

10

The Responsibilities of Believers
Colossians 3:18—4:6

Corporate oneness in position does not abrogate individual responsibility and function. Racial, social, and sexual distinctions remain, even though there is equality in Christ. In this new section, Paul sought to apply the general principles of Christian behavior to specific life situations.

I. IN THE HOME (3:18—4:1)

God created the original home when He brought Adam and Eve together. The home existed before the church, and it continues to function as the foundation of local congregations. The purpose of the church, therefore, is to complement the family and to honor the unique responsibilities of each member of the household. There must not be any contradiction in function, or role reversal. In other words, it is not possible for a male to be the authoritative head of the family and for a female to be the ruling officer of the local church. The principles and responsibilities specified for family members must carry over into the church, which is the extension of the family.

In this section, the duties of six family members are set forth. Those duties are stated in three pairs of sentences. In each pair, the subordinate person is addressed first.

THE RESPONSIBILITIES OF BELIEVERS

A. Wives (3:18)

The term used in the address *(hai gunaikes)*[1] can refer either to a female in contrast to a male (Matt. 9:20) or to a wife (Matt. 5:28). In this context, it points to the latter.

1. The command

The imperative *(hupotassesthe)* can be translated in two possible ways: "submit yourselves" or "be submissive."[2] In either case, the present tense stresses constant, daily submission. The word comes from the military world where soldiers were to be in order *(tassō)* under *(hupo)* the directions of their officer. Paul earlier praised the Colossians' spiritual order (2:5).

The subordination of the wife to the husband, both in the family and in the church, is functional. It is intended to help believers carry out the divine purpose for the family. It does not imply personal inferiority or dictatorial rule. Paul explained: "But I would have you know, that the head of every man is Christ, and the head of the woman is the man, and the head of Christ is God" (I Cor. 11:3). Within the trinitarian oneness of the divine Being, there is an equality of persons, but there is also a functional order to execute the redemptive program. In like manner, the husband and the wife are personal equals, but there is subordination for functional purposes.

The headship of the man is based on two truths: the order of creation (I Tim. 2:13) and the judgment imposed on the woman for her deception in the temptation (I Tim. 2:14). After the original sin, God said to Eve: ". . . and thy desire shall be to thy husband, and he shall rule over thee" (Gen. 3:16). Until the establishment of the eternal state, this order must be observed on earth in the family and in the church.

Submission involves both love and obedience (Titus 2:4–5). It should mark the godly wife even if her husband is not saved (I Peter 3:1–6).

---

[1] The term *gynecologist* is based on this word.
[2] The first identifies the verb in the middle voice; the second in the passive. Both voices in the present tense use the same Greek ending.

2. *The reason*

The reason for such submission is "as it is fit in the Lord." Literally, it translates "it was fitting" *(anēken)*.[3] Subordination befits Christian women. God established the authority of family function in the Garden of Eden. The entrance of sin or the salvation experience have not changed that basic principle. It is not a cultural oddity which can be altered in different countries and ages.

B. Husbands (3:19)

The term used in the address *(hoi andres)* can refer either to the male in contrast to a female (Matt. 15:38) or to a husband (Matt. 1:19). In this context, it points to the latter. Two commands are issued to husbands.

1. *Love*

The directive *(agapate)* calls for continuous love, at all times and in all situations.[4] The husband should love his wife "even as Christ also loved the church, and gave himself for it" (Eph. 5:25). Christ's love is a sacrificial love, a giving love, an altruistic love, a holy and redemptive love. It is a nourishing and cherishing love, a love which makes its object feel valuable and wanted (Eph. 5:26–27). Such love forgives, sanctifies, and cleanses.

2. *Be not bitter*

When love weakens, bitterness sets in. The negative command, "be not bitter against them," warns against this threat to a strong biblical, sociological marriage. Bitterness is the opposite of sweetness (Rev. 8:11; 10:9). The imperative *(pikrainesthe)* stresses the constant prevention of this sour attitude. A bitter husband will become a harsh, unscrupulous dictator. He looks on his wife simply as a servant, an object to satisfy his petty whims.

Elsewhere, Peter advised: "Likewise, ye husbands, dwell with them according to knowledge, giving honour unto the wife, as unto the weaker vessel, and as being heirs together of the grace

---

[3] Imperfect active indicative.
[4] Present active imperative.

of life, that your prayers be not hindered" (I Peter 3:7). A loving husband understands his wife. He seeks to meet her needs (I Cor. 7:3). He also appreciates her; he treats her with respect. On the other hand, discord severs personal communication and produces an ineffective prayer life.

C. Children (3:20)

"Children" *(ta tekna)* embraces those who are still dependent on their parents for their daily physical needs. They have not yet married nor have they reached that designated time when their parents view them as legal adults (Gal. 4:1–2). A young man was regarded as a child until he became a son in the official sense with all the privileges and responsibilities pertaining thereto.

1. The command

The command has three features. *First,* a child must obey constantly.[5] The imperative *(hupakouete)* literally means "to hear" *(akouō)* "under" *(hupo).* A child who obeys is one who puts himself under the authority of his parents, listens to the parental directives, and does as he is told, without complaint and rebellion.

Second, obedience must be toward both "parents." This fact implies that both parents agree about what is expected of their children. If the father and the mother give contradictory commands, it is impossible for the child to comply with the divine imperative. Each parent can give a separate charge, but it must be done with the full support of the other. The context implies that these are saved parents (3:21).

Third, obedience extends to "all things." This includes all aspects of daily life: work, play, church, and social activities.

2. The reason

Obedience of children is "well pleasing unto the Lord." Whatever children do, they should also do for the glory of the Lord (3:17). Submission to parental authority is a sign of submission to God. Elsewhere Paul wrote:

[5] Present active imperative.

> Children, obey your parents in the Lord: for this is right. Honor thy father and mother; which is the first commandment with promise;
>
> That it may be well with thee, and thou mayest live long on the earth (Eph. 6:1–3).

The fifth of the Ten Commandments, quoted here, recognized the divine authority of parental rule within the family structure (Exod. 20:12). The child who obeys acknowledges that chain of command.

D. Parents (3:21)

The direct address, "Fathers" *(hoi pateres)*, could refer to the male parent only, but it more likely applies to both the father and mother (Heb. 11:23).[6] The father is the authoritative head of the family, but the mother also "guides the house" (I Tim. 5:14).

1. The command

The negative command actually constitutes a warning: "Provoke not your children . . . lest. . . ." The imperative *(erethizete)* means "to excite" or "to stimulate." Some provocation can be good and necessary; the willingness of the Corinthians to give money provoked other churches to contribute likewise (II Cor. 9:2). The usual result of bad provocation, however, is strife *(eritheiai)*, a work of the sinful flesh and a display of carnality (I Cor. 3:3; Gal. 5:20). Since like begets like, a parent who provokes will produce a child of strife. Such provocation makes unreasonable demands on the child, humiliates him, and manifests no loving understanding of his unique personality. It is marked by constant nagging.

The remedy is a positive approach: ". . . but bring them up in the nurture and admonition of the Lord" (Eph. 6:4). A godly parent must warn and teach, but he must be sure that he is communicating the divine will and not his own petty convictions.

---

[6]The Greek word usually denotes the father *(patēr)* in contrast to the mother *(mētēr)*. The word, however is rightly translated as "parents" when Moses was hidden by them (Heb. 11:23).

2. The reason

The children should not "be discouraged" *(athumōsin)*. It literally means "no wrath." Its stem contains the same word that was translated as "wrath," an emotional sin which should be put off (3:8). Wrong provocation, however, can quench any vital emotional expression within a child. Emotions must not be eliminated; rather, they must be guided and sanctified. A discouraged child has no spirit; he has "a sullen, listless, discouraged disposition."[7] This child has no spirit, no desire to become what God wants him to be.

E. Servants (3:22–25)

More space and attention are given to the responsibilities of slaves than to the combined responsibilities of husbands, wives, parents, and children. One reason was the return to Colosse of Onesimus, the runaway slave who was now a believer (4:9). Another is the fact that many Christians were slaves, a class which constituted almost one-half of the population of the Roman empire.

The address "servants" can better be translated as "slaves" *(hoi douloi)*. These people were not freemen who were household workers. They were owned as chattel property, to be bought and sold. People became slaves by being born of slave parents, through financial loss, or by military conquest.

1. The commands (3:22–23)

Two commands are given. *First,* the slave must obey his human master. The imperative "obey" *(hupakouete)* stresses constant, daily obedience.[8] This obedience extends to "all things," both those which the slaves like to do and those which are unpleasant. Obedience must be rendered to slaves' human owners and foremen ("masters according to the flesh.") These masters could either be saved or unsaved. The spiritual condition of the

---

[7] Homer A. Kent, Jr., *Treasures of Wisdom: Studies in Colossians and Philemon*, p. 130.

[8] Present active imperative. It is the same verb as that used for the children.

owner was to have no effect on the quality of the slave's work. The term "masters" *(kurioi)* is later translated as "Lord" in reference to Christ (3:23–24).

Mere obedience, however, is not sufficient. Its manner is just as important. This is indicated in two ways: negatively and positively, before men and before God. Work must not be done "with eyeservice, as menpleasers" (cf. Eph. 6:5–8). The person who does this works only when he is being watched and works only enough to satisfy the minimum demands of his master. Rather, this obedience must be given "in singleness of heart, fearing God." The noun "singleness" *(haplotēti)* literally means "without a fold." It denotes that everything is seen and that no misdeed or faulty motive is hidden by duplicity. It is the "opposite of double-dealing and hypocrisy."[9] With a full understanding that God sees both the action and the attitude and that God sees when men are not present, the godly slave will perform his task to the best of his ability in order to be a good testimony for Christ.

Second, the slave must work for God. The imperative "do" *(ergazesthe)* denotes faithful toil and labor.[10] Four features of this work are listed. First, it covers all of his assigned responsibilities ("and whatsoever ye do"). Second, it must be done with total enthusiasm. The adverb "heartily" translates a prepositional phrase which literally reads "out of soul" *(ek psuchēs)*. Such labor must not be cold and perfunctory; rather, it should be warm and emotional. Third, it should be done "as to the Lord." Fourth, it should not be performed merely "unto men." Thus, labor is a sacred service even when it is executed in the context of first-century slavery. It is doing the will of God with good human will (Eph. 6:6–7).

2. The reasons (3:24–25)

The participle, "knowing," introduces two reasons for the slaves' obedience and work. *First,* faithful service will receive a divine "reward" (3:24). If a slave actually serves Christ in his menial tasks, the Savior will reward him at the judgment seat in

---

[9] Kent, *Treasures of Wisdom,* p. 131.

[10] Present middle imperative.

heaven (II Cor. 5:10). In real life, a slave received no wages or an inheritance; but in the spiritual life, the slave is entitled to all of the blessings of his heavenly inheritance which Christ has provided. Rewards, however, are not given to make up for inequities on earth. All Christians, regardless of their human status, must labor with clean hands and hearts in order to be honored in that future day of examination.

Second, poor service will be judged (3:25).[11] To do "wrong" *(adikōn)* is to do that which does not conform to the righteous character and standards of a just God. Such wrongdoing involves doing less than one's best, doing the minimum rather than the maximum, doing to impress, and doing it apart from the heart. Slaves can fool their earthly masters, but they cannot deceive God.

Before God, "there is no respect of persons." At the judgment seat, the slave will not receive preferential treatment because he had a difficult life on earth. The judgment in that day will be of man's faithfulness and spirituality, not of racial distinctions or social deprivation. God will treat all believers alike: the slave and the master, the man and the woman, the Jew and the Gentile, and the rich and the poor. A slave who does wrong will suffer the same judgment as the master who does wrong.

F. Masters (4:1)

In this section (3:22—4:1), the Greek term is translated in the plural as "masters" *(hoi kurioi)* and in the singular as both "master" and "lord" *(kurios)*. The former refers to the earthly owners of slaves (3:22; 4:1) and the latter to the Lord Jesus Christ (3:23, 24; 4:1). The masters referred to in this address are definitely believers, as was Philemon (Philem. 16). Masters constitute the sixth group in Paul's description of the church membership at Colosse.

---

[11] It is debatable whether this verse pertains to the slave (Peake, Lenski), the master (Abbott, Carson), or to both (Lightfoot, Hendriksen). The general principle applies to both, but its primary application here is to the slave.

1. The command

Masters are charged to "give" daily *(parechesthe)* two things to their slaves.[12] *First,* masters should render "that which is just" *(to dikaion).* If a master refuses to do this, then he actually does "wrong" *(adikon;* 3:25) and he will be judged by God for this sin. A just recompense is legally and morally right; it corresponds to the righteous character of God.

Second, masters should give that which is "equal" *(tēn isotēta).*[13] Various interpretations of this concept have been suggested. First, it implies the emancipation of the slaves. Second, masters should carry out their responsibilities to their slaves equally as well as the slaves serve the masters (cf. Eph. 6:8–9). Third, they should treat their slaves in the same way that God has treated them.[14] Fourth, it denotes the equality of spiritual brotherhood. Fifth, it may indicate that a master should not give one slave more and another less for doing the same job with comparable excellence. In this sense, he should not show respect of persons.

2. The reason

All Christians, including both slaves and masters, know that they have a heavenly master, the Lord Jesus Christ. Masters will one day give an account to Him for how they have treated other men. In the performance of their duties, they must also practice the principles of the new man. They must recognize that they are also spiritual slaves to Christ and that they must willingly serve the needs of others. Although Paul never clearly condemned the institution of slavery, he did set forth principles which would eventually lead to its elimination, at least by dedicated believers.

II. IN THE WORLD (4:2–6)

The major didactic section of the epistle ends with these clos-

---

[12]The two direct objects are very emphatic, occurring at the very beginning of the verse.

[13]The usage of two separate definite articles with the nouns shows that these are two distinct entities.

[14]Author's view.

ing admonitions to all segments of the church membership. Regardless of family or social status, all believers have responsibilities toward all men. In the execution of household duties, these must not be neglected.

A. Prayer (4:2–4)

Prayer is the very breath of spirituality. Its absence indicates deadness and coldness. Two of its motivations are concern for self and intercession for others. It is not wrong to pray for oneself; in fact, Christ even prayed for Himself before He prayed for others (John 17). In this section, the apostle wanted the Colossian believers to pray for themselves and then for him.

1. For self (4:2)

Three elements constitute this command. *First,* the Colossian believers should "continue in prayer."[15] The imperative *(proskartereite)* means to devote one's time, attention, and strength to a task. This diligence in prayer was characteristic of the apostles (Acts 1:14; 6:4), the first three thousand converts (Acts 2:42), and the Roman Christians (Rom. 12:12). Elsewhere, Paul counseled: "Praying always with all prayer and supplication in the Spirit, and watching thereunto with all perseverance [same word] and supplication for all saints" (Eph. 6:18). The believer must pray without ceasing (I Thess. 5:17). It is part of the Christian's offensive and defensive armor in his spiritual battle with the forces of evil.

Second, the Colossians should "watch" in their prayer life. In Gethsemane, Christ cautioned His disciples: "Watch and pray, that ye enter not into temptation: the spirit indeed is willing, but the flesh is weak" (Matt. 26:41). He wanted them to watch with Him, not for Him (Matt. 26:38). Watchfulness involves mental alertness and spiritual vigilance, a sensitive awareness that one is in danger. Peter, who was justly criticized in the garden, later warned: "Be sober, be vigilant; because your adversary the devil, as a roaring lion, walketh about, seeking whom he may devour"

---

[15] Actually, this is the only Greek imperative in the verse. The directive "watch" *(grēgorountes)* is a participle.

(I Peter 5:8). The Colossians needed to know that the heretical teachers were actually the ministers of Satan (II Cor. 11:14).

Third, these believers should pray "with thanksgiving." A believer must express gratitude to the God of peace for the peace which God gives and which stands as a sentry around his heart and mind (Phil. 4:6). Thanksgiving acknowledges submission to the will of God (I Thess. 5:18).

2. *For Paul (4:3–4)*

Since Christ was God manifest in the flesh, He never asked anyone to pray for Him. Paul, however, knew that he needed the intercession of others even though he was a mature, spiritual believer. Paul requested such prayer from the church when it was engaged in worshipful prayer and intercession for others ("withal praying also for us"). The term "withal" *(hama)* means "together with, at the same time." Prayer for him was to be additional, not substitutional.

The apostle made two requests, indicated by the double usage of "that." *First,* he desired an opportunity for witness. He was a missionary evangelist, first and foremost. Actually, the petition was also for Timothy and his other associates in Rome ("us"; cf. 1:1; 4:7–14). The prayer's immediate goal was "that God would open unto us a door of utterance."[16] Prayer does not open doors, but a God who answers prayer does. When He opens up the door for service, no sinner can shut it; when He closes the door, no saint can open it (Rev. 3:7–8). Ephesus in Asia was a closed door to Paul during his second preaching journey (Acts 16:6), but it was opened as a great and effectual door during his third trip (I Cor. 16:9). Later, God opened another door for evangelism at Troas (II Cor. 2:12). The joint prayer of the Colossians and the Ephesians was answered because members of Caesar's military guard and household became believers through the apostle's testimony (Eph. 6:19–20; Phil. 1:13; 4:22). The spiritual depth of Paul can be seen here in the fact that he desired an opportunity for witness rather than a release from his imprisonment. He was more concerned for others than for himself.

---

[16] Literally, it reads "a door for the word" *(thuran tou logou).*

Paul's ultimate purpose was "to speak the mystery of Christ" (1:26–27; 2:2).[17] The truth that both Jew and Gentile become one in Christ through saving faith formed the content of his message. In essence, Christ was the mystery: who He is, what He did at the cross, and what He was doing through His body, the church. The cause of Paul's imprisonment was the fact that he refused to preach a Judaistic gospel, complete with circumcision and legalism ("for which I am also in bonds"). When the Jews seized him in the temple at Jerusalem, they falsely accused him: "Men of Israel, help: This is the man, that teacheth all men everywhere against the people, and the law, and this place" (Acts 21:28). When he arrived in Rome, the Jews of that city acknowledged that the "sect" of Christians was "spoken against" (Acts 28:22). When Christ Himself spoke of divine blessing conferred on Gentiles rather than on Jews, the Jews in the Nazareth synagogue almost killed him out of intense rage and hatred (Luke 4:16–30).

Second, Paul desired an effective witness (4:4). It is one thing for God to open a door of witness; it is another for a believer to enter it. Three years before, God directly encouraged him: "Be of good cheer, Paul: for as thou hast testified of me in Jerusalem, so must thou bear witness also at Rome" (Acts 23:11). Now, at Rome, Paul hoped: "That I may make it manifest, as I ought to speak." God manifested the hidden mystery to him shortly after his conversion (1:26), but now he had the privilege and responsibility to make it clear to sinners and believers. He had no options; he was under obligation to preach. Elsewhere he testified: "For though I preach the gospel, I have nothing to glory of: for necessity is laid upon me; yea, woe is unto me, if I preach not the gospel" (I Cor. 9:16).

B. Witness (4:5–6)

Unsaved men watch and listen; therefore, a Christian must be consistent in what he does and what he says. Lest he be called a hypocrite, there must be a holy balance between life and lip. Paul encouraged the church to exercise this double witness.

---

[17]The relative pronoun "which" *(ho)* agrees with its antecedent, "mystery." Both are in the neuter gender.

STAND PERFECT IN WISDOM

1. Walk (4:5)

Four features can be seen in a God-pleasing walk. *First,* it must be a consistent, daily walk. The imperative, "walk" *(peripateite),* views the Christian life in its total aspects and application.[18] Earlier, Paul prayed that the Colossians might have a worthy walk (1:10; 2:6).

Second, this walk must be "in wisdom." Great stress is placed upon this manner of the walk.[19] Spiritual wisdom begins with a genuine fear of God and ends with the exaltation of Christ (2:3; Prov. 1:7). It must be in total conformity to the will of God revealed in the Scriptures (1:9–10). The heretics boasted about their love of wisdom, but genuine wisdom is seen in a godly life under the control of the Holy Spirit.

Third, the outreach is "toward them that are without" *(pros tous exō).* Harrison said that this terminology "was both a lament and a challenge."[20] It definitely refers to the world of unsaved men (I Cor. 5:12; I Thess. 4:12; I Tim. 3:7). They are outside of the true church and Christ; they are hopeless and "without God in the world" (Eph. 2:12). If they are not saved, they will be outside the holy city, the habitation of the redeemed, for all eternity (Rev. 22:15).

Fourth, its urgency is contained in the participial phrase, "redeeming the time." All have the same amount of time; the clock is no respecter of persons. The child of God, however, must "buy out" *(exagorazomenoi)* opportunities whereby he may reach the lost with an effective witness. This compulsion recognizes that "the days are evil" (Eph. 5:16).

2. Speech (4:6)

The tongue is the most difficult member of the body to control (James 3:1–10). It can produce either blessing or cursing. The concept of "speech" *(logos)* includes both the content and the manner of oral expression. Four characteristics of proper speech for the believer are stated here. *First,* it must be consistent ("al-

---

[18] Present active imperative.
[19] Literally, it reads: "In wisdom walk."
[20] Everett F. Harrison, *Colossians: Christ All-sufficient,* p. 106.

way"). At all times and under all situations, it should be the same.

Second, the believer must speak "with grace." In the face of open hostility, the believer must address the unsaved in a way which the latter does not deserve; the Christian must manifest a winsomeness. Christ spoke "gracious words" to the synagogue worshipers at Nazareth who shortly thereafter would try to kill him (Luke 4:22).

Third, the Christian's speech must be "seasoned with salt." Salt enhances flavor and makes food appetizing. Too much or too little makes the food unpalatable. Salt also retards corruption. The Christian must give an oral witness in such a way that he shows disapproval of sin on the one hand and graciously seeks to win the sinner on the other. In essence, he must hate the sin and love the sinner at the same time. He must speak "that which is good to the use of edifying, that it may minister grace unto the hearers" (Eph. 4:29).

Fourth, speech must manifest a sensitivity and awareness to the needs of each individual. Although all the unsaved are equally lost, they still exist as distinctive personalities. A Christian cannot use the same evangelistic technique each time, although the redemptive content of the message must never be altered. He must "know how [he] ought to answer every man." This knowledge can be gained only through spiritual and mental preparation and a humble submission to the Spirit (I Peter 3:15).

Questions for Discussion

1. Why are wives afraid to submit to their husbands? How can wives contribute effectively to family leadership?

2. How can a husband show that he loves his wife? How can he become more sensitive to her needs?

3. To what extent should saved children obey their unsaved parents? When do they cease being children?

4. How can parents discourage their children? Discuss these principles, and give practical suggestions for avoiding this fault.

5. How can the slave-master relationship be transferred into the modern world of employee-employer? How should Christians conduct their businesses?

6. How strong is evangelical prayer life today? How strong is your prayer life? How can it be improved?

7. How can believers redeem opportunities for witness? at work? at school? on vacation?

11

The Blessing of Friends
Colossians 4:7–18

Solomon wrote that "a friend loveth at all times" (Prov. 17:17). Friends encourage and stand by each other in difficult days (Prov. 27:6, 10, 17). A man who has them is rich indeed.

In this closing section, Paul mentioned eleven personal acquaintances who had been a blessing to him.

I. HIS REPRESENTATIVES (4:7–9)

Paul sent two representatives to the church at Colosse. The first was the bearer of the epistle, and the second was returning to his master, Philemon.

A. Tychicus (4:7–8)

1. His life

His name means "fortuitous" or "fortunate." He is mentioned five times in the New Testament. A native of the Roman province of Asia, Tychicus accompanied Paul into that region at the end of the apostle's third journey (Acts 20:4). He was with the apostle during the latter's first Roman imprisonment (Eph. 6:21; Col. 4:7). He was given the responsibility of delivering three of Paul's prison epistles (Ephesians, Colossians, and Philemon).[1] Since he was from Asia, he was a logical choice for this task. Subsequently,

---

[1] Four, if the Laodicean letter was not one of these.

he traveled with the apostle after the latter's acquittal and probably went to Crete as the replacement for Titus (Titus 3:12). He later reappeared in Rome when Paul was imprisoned there a second time, but the apostle sent Tychicus to Ephesus shortly before his martyrdom (II Tim. 4:12).

2. His character

Three positive commendations are stated. *First*, Tychicus was a "beloved brother." He was a spiritual brother, both to Paul and the members of the Colossian church. They and all the other believers loved him.

Second, Tychicus was a "faithful minister." He served as Paul's apostolic representative several times and executed his responsibilities well. Paul could count on him without question. Nothing negative about Tychicus is stated in Scripture.

Third, he was a "fellowservant." Paul, Timothy, and Tychicus were joined together in loving service to their heavenly master, the Lord Jesus Christ. As spiritual slaves, they submitted their wills and ambitions to Him.

All three designations were "in the Lord" (Eph. 6:21). In real life, Tychicus was not a slave or a natural brother to the apostle.

3. His purpose

Paul "sent" *(epempsa)*[2] Tychicus for three reasons. *First*, Tychicus was to inform the church about the circumstances surrounding the apostle's imprisonment ("all my state").[3] This same phrase is used elsewhere of his predicament and is translated in several ways: "cause" (Acts 25:14); "my affairs" (Eph. 6:21); and "the things which happened unto me" (Phil. 1:12). In its concerns, the church had sent Epaphras to Rome to get firsthand information, but he was imprisoned also (Philem. 23). Tychicus thus made known how God had used the imprisonment to advance the gospel message (Phil. 1:12).

Second, Tychicus was to ascertain the spiritual health of the

---

[2] Epistolary aorist. He was not yet sent at the time of writing, but he had already been sent at the time of reading.

[3] Literally, "the things according to me."

church ("that he might know your estate").[4] Paul wanted to know how much damage had been done since the departure of Epaphras. It apparently was the responsibility of Tychicus to give additional correction, admonition, and instruction. Since Paul expected an imminent release from his imprisonment (Phil. 2:24; Philem. 22), he did not plan for his associate to report to him in the imperial city.

Third, Tychicus was to "comfort [their] hearts." The Colossians were undoubtedly anxious about the imprisonments of Paul and Epaphras, the confusion and dissension which the heresy produced, and the future vitality of the church. Encouragement and comfort come from concerned, involved friends and from a thorough knowledge of the facts.

B. Onesimus (4:9)

1. His life

His name occurs only twice in the biblical record (4:9; Philem. 10). He was an unsaved slave of a Christian master, Philemon. After Onesimus had wronged his master, he ran away to Rome, where he encountered Paul in prison. Through the witness of the apostle, Onesimus became a believer. Subsequently, Paul sent him back to Philemon under the custody of Tychicus, who was going to Colosse with the epistles. Further information about Onesimus can be gained through a study of the Book of Philemon.

2. His character (4:9a)

Paul described Onesimus in four ways. *First,* he was a "brother." In Christ, he had become a spiritual brother to Paul, Timothy, the associates in Rome, the church at Colosse, and even Philemon, his master (Philem. 16). They had all partaken of the divine nature by their new birth (John 1:12–13).

Second, Onesimus was "faithful." At Rome, he was known for his life of faith and for his faithful service to the apostle. In do-

---

[4]The critical Greek text reads, "that you might know the things concerning us."

mestic duties, he ministered to the apostle and proved to be very profitable (Philem. 11, 13).

Third, Onesimus was "beloved" by Paul, the associates, and by the Roman church. Now, the apostle wanted both Philemon and the Colossian church to confer such Christian love upon him (Philem. 16). To Paul, both Tychicus and Onesimus were equally beloved brothers.

Fourth, Onesimus was from Colosse ("who is one of you"). Actually, this phrase denotes more than just his geographical origin. In Paul's viewpoint, Onesimus was now a member of the church at Colosse (cf. 4:12).

3. His purpose (4:9b)

Both Tychicus and Onesimus informed the church about the situation of Paul in Rome. In this sense, they were equal apostolic representatives.

II. HIS ASSOCIATES (4:10–14)

In this section, seven people are mentioned. With the exception of Barnabas, six were associated with Paul in his imprisonment and limited ministry at Rome. They are identified in two ways. *First*, they were his "fellowworkers unto the kingdom of God" (4:11). They were all born again by faith and thus they had entered the spiritual realm of the kingdom of God (1:13; John 3:3–5). In addition, they worked with each other and with the apostle to bring others into the same salvation experience.

Second, these associates had become "a comfort" to Paul in the difficulties of his confinement. The Greek word for "comfort" (*parēgoria*) has been transliterated into the English as "paregoric," a medicine which brings relief from pain. They undoubtedly performed this ministry of caring by their mere presence and conversation, by their willingness to stand with him in the pagan court, by their financial help, and by their evangelistic outreach at Rome. Paul earlier received such encouragement when the ship which carried him to Rome made a brief stop at Sidon. There the Roman centurion "gave him liberty to go unto his friends to refresh himself" (Acts 27:3). Solomon wisely and correctly observed: "Iron sharpeneth iron; so man sharpeneth the countenance of his friend" (Prov. 27:17).

A. Jewish Workers (4:10–11)

Spiritual oneness in Christ can be seen in the fact that Jewish and Gentile believers worked beside Paul and that both groups wanted to salute the church at Colosse. The first three men were "of the circumcision" *(hoi ontes ek peritomēs)*.[5] They were Jewish, circumcised when they were infants, raised in legalistic Judaism, and had been saved. Their background and conversion corresponded to that of Paul (Phil. 3:4–6).

1. Aristarchus (4:10a)

His name means "ruler of the dinner." He was a Jew who lived in Thessalonica (Acts 20:4; 27:2). He may have been converted to Christ during Paul's evangelistic work in that city during the apostle's second journey (Acts 17:1–10). He first appears in the biblical record as a traveling companion of Paul during the apostle's ministry in Ephesus on his third journey (Acts 19:29). At that time Aristarchus and Gaius were almost martyred by the pagan silversmiths who had dragged the pair into the amphitheater before an angry mob. Along with others, he moved with Paul into Macedonia, Achaia, back to Macedonia, and on to Asia at the end of the third apostolic journey (Acts 20:4). The Bible is silent as to whether he traveled with Paul to Jerusalem; however, he was with the apostle in Rome (4:10; Philem. 24).

Aristarchus is further identified here as Paul's "fellowprisoner." This descriptive title may mean that he actually was under house arrest in Rome with the apostle or that he had been in jail at some time in the past for his faith in Christ (cf. Rom. 16:7). Since the evangelists considered themselves to be soldiers for Christ (Phil. 2:25), Paul may have seen Aristarchus as a spiritual captive of war. He thus voluntarily identified himself with the real prisoner, the apostle Paul.

---

[5] Both a plural relative pronoun and participle are used here.

2. Mark (4:10b)

His given name was John, and his Latin surname was Mark. His mother was Mary, a resident of Jerusalem and a relative of Barnabas. Mark was either a cousin or a nephew to Barnabas (ho anepsios).[6] The family apparently had some wealth (Acts 4:37; 12:12). He may have been the young man who followed Jesus after His arrest in Gethsemane and who later fled naked (Mark 14:51–52).[7]

His home was the site for the prayer meeting in which the believers requested the release of Peter (Acts 12:12–17). He may have been a direct convert of Peter, because that apostle later identified Mark as his spiritual son (I Peter 5:13).

Mark's active ministry began when he accompanied Paul and Barnabas in the early stages of the first missionary journey (Acts 12:25; 13:1–13); however, he returned to Jerusalem without completing the trip. At the beginning of the second journey, Paul and Barnabas disagreed over the advisability of giving Mark a second opportunity (Acts 15:36–41). The Bible is silent about his activities during the next ten years.

The differences between Mark and Paul must have been resolved, because the former was with the apostle during the first Roman imprisonment (4:10; Philem. 24). They were fellow workers in the gospel. Much later, during Paul's second Roman imprisonment, he asked Timothy to bring Mark "for he is profitable to me for the ministry" (II Tim. 4:11). Mark thus had matured in both faith and service, having overcome his early failures. In fact, he became the author of the second Gospel which therefore bears his name.

The church "received commandments" concerning Mark. There is no indication of any prior communication between Paul and the church; Tychicus probably transmitted some oral directives.[8]

The possibility of a future visit to Colosse by Mark is implied in

---

[6] The term can be understood in either way. The word "sister" does not appear in the Greek text.

[7] This speculation is based upon the fact that only the Gospel of Mark contains this account.

[8] The verb could be an epistolary aorist (cf. 4:8, "sent").

the conditional clause ("if he come unto you"). If that should occur, the church was to give Mark a hospitable reception ("receive him").

3. Jesus Justus

The given name of this Jew was "Jesus" *(Iēsous)*, the Greek equivalent for the Hebrew Joshua. It is the oldest name containing the divine name Yahweh. It therefore means "Yahweh is help" or "Yahweh is salvation." Both the Jews of Palestine and of the dispersion often gave this name to their male children.

Since the name Jesus is revered by the Christian as distinctively His, this Jew probably changed his name to Justus after his conversion. All that is known of him is found in this verse. He was a Jew ("of the circumcision"), a fellow worker, and a source of comfort to Paul.

Two other men in the New Testament bear the name of Justus, but this man should not be identified with either. One was an early disciple who was considered as the replacement for Judas in the apostolic group (Acts 1:23). The other was a Corinthian whose home became the meeting place for believers after Paul left the synagogue (Acts 18:7).

B. Gentile Workers (4:12–14)

The concluding statement about the first group of three Jewish associates also serves as a transition to the second group of three Gentile workers (4:11b).

1. Epaphras (4:12–13)

His name appears three times in the Biblical record (1:7; 4:12; Philem. 23). Four aspects of his life and ministry are given here. *First,* Epaphras was from the church at Colosse ("who is one of you"). He may have been the founder of the church; if not, he definitely was its main pastor-teacher (1:7). He traveled to Rome to inquire about Paul and to inform the apostle about the spiritual condition of the Colossian believers (1:8).

Second, Epaphras was "a servant of Christ." Earlier, Paul called him "our dear fellowservant" (1:7). This complimentary title was used elsewhere only of Timothy (Phil. 1:1). He was a true spiritual slave whose will was totally submissive to that of Christ.

Third, Epaphras was a prayer warrior. His prayers were intense and persistent ("always laboring fervently for you in prayers"). Four features of his prayer ministry can be deduced from this verse. First, his prayers were constant and frequent ("always"). Second, they involved the effort of his total being. The participle "laboring fervently" *(agōnizomenos)* stresses the expenditure of physical energy. It involves the struggle of the mind and the emotions (cf. 1:29). He shared Paul's "conflict" *(agōna;* 2:1) over the heretical threat to the church. Third, the prayers were intercessory ("for you"). Although Epaphras was himself in prison, he was concerned about his spiritual children in Colosse. Fourth, his prayers were specific and purposeful. He requested that the Colossians might "stand perfect and complete in all the will of God." The "stand" refers to their doctrinal integrity and basis of Christian behavior. He did not want them to submit to the deceitful influence of the heretics, especially now that he knew from Paul how dangerous the false teaching really was. Since he was confined to house arrest, he had to wage his spiritual battle through prayer. He wanted them to have a "perfect" *(teleioi)* stand; thus he joined with Paul in a desire to present every man "perfect in Christ Jesus" (1:28). He desired for them to become what God had willed for them; he wanted them to achieve their goals here on earth. He also wanted them to have a "complete" *(peplērōmenoi)* stand.[9] Positionally, they were already complete in Christ (2:10), but they needed to become convinced of their total acceptance in the Savior. Their doctrinal convictions needed to become fully established so that they would resist any pressure of error.

Fourth, Epaphras had compassionate concern for the spiritual welfare of believers in his native region (4:13). Paul observed this commendable trait and transmitted it to the church ("For I bear him record"). He had "great zeal" *(zēlon polun),* a holy jealousy over them (cf. II Cor. 11:2).[10] It hurt him to see the believers

---

[9] The critical Greek text uses "fully assured" *(peplērophorēmenoi).*

[10] The critical Greek text used "pain" *(ponon).*

being misled into error. This burden extended to three groups of Christians: ". . . for you, and them that are in Laodicea, and them in Hierapolis." These cities were clustered together geographically and joined together spiritually. What affected one affected the others. It is plausible that Epaphras might have evangelized the entire territory and that he started churches in two of them (4:15–16).

The church at Laodicea endured this crisis and still was in existence at the end of the first century (Rev. 1:1; 3:14–22). It prospered financially, but became spiritually bankrupt in the course of the years. Christ warned it severely when He sent one of the seven letters to it. Since it is mentioned as one of the seven key churches of Asia, it probably supplanted the church at Colosse in ecclesiastical influence.

This is the only mention of Hierapolis in the entire New Testament.

2. Luke

Luke is mentioned only three times, each time in Paul's epistles (4:14; II Tim. 4:11; Philem. 24); however, his life and ministry can be discovered through a correlation of the Book of Acts with the epistles of Paul.[11]

Luke joined the missionary team of Paul, Silas, and Timothy at Troas and journeyed with them to Philippi (Acts 16:10–39). When the team left for Thessalonica, Luke remained behind in Philippi, possibly to oversee the young church and to practice medicine. At the conclusion of his third journey, Paul again traveled into Macedonia where Luke joined him once more at Philippi (Acts 20:1–6). From that point on, Luke was Paul's constant companion, possibly to minister to the apostle's physical needs. He went with Paul from Philippi to Troas, Miletus, Tyre, Caesarea, and Jerusalem, where the apostle was arrested (Acts 20:6—21:17).

When the Romans took Paul from Jerusalem to Caesarea, where he was imprisoned for two years, Luke went also. During

---

[11] Indicated by the "we" and "us" sections in Acts. The author inserted himself into the action at these points.

this period, Luke gathered information and wrote the third Gospel.

Luke was with Paul during the troubled voyage from Caesarea to Puteoli in Italy (Acts 27:1—28:13). He remained with Paul during his two years of house arrest in Rome (4:14; Acts 28:14–31; Philem. 24). At this time, Luke finished writing the Book of Acts.

It is generally agreed that Paul was released from this first Roman internment; however, Paul was later arrested and brought to a Roman jail for the second time. Since Luke was again with Paul during this second confinement (II Tim. 4:11), it is safe to conclude that he also traveled with the apostle during the interval between the two Roman imprisonments. As his martyrdom approached, Paul plainly reported: "Only Luke is with me" (II Tim. 4:11).

This physician proved to be a beloved, faithful friend.

3. Demas

Demas is mentioned three times in the New Testament (4:14; II Tim. 4:10; Philem. 24). Although his name is listed last here, it appears between the names of Aristarchus and Luke elsewhere (Philem. 24). At this time in his life, he was a "fellowlabourer" (Philem. 24) with Paul and the other associates.

In the interval between Paul's two Roman imprisonments, Demas may have traveled with the apostle, because he was with Paul at the beginning of the second confinement. Unfortunately, however, a spiritual weakness surfaced in his life. Paul sadly wrote about him: "For Demas hath forsaken me, having loved this present world, and is departed unto Thessalonica" (II Tim. 4:10). This defection prompted an urgent appeal to Timothy to join the apostle in his last days (II Tim. 4:9).

III. HIS READERS (4:15–18)

The closing words of the epistle contain a salutation, counsel, a prayer request, and a blessing.

THE BLESSING OF FRIENDS

A. At Laodicea (4:15-16)

1. The brethren (4:15a)

The Colossians served as intermediaries for the apostle. They were to perform a service for him. He asked them to "salute the brethren which are in Laodicea." This phrase describes the total group of believers in that city, those who constituted the local manifestation of the body of Christ, the true church.

2. Nymphas (4:15b)

This is the only mention of Nymphas in the Scriptures.[12] Since his name is given, he must have been an influential believer, perhaps the pastor of the congregation which met in his home.

3. The church (4:15c)

In the first century, believers met in private homes for worship and fellowship (Acts 12:12; 16:40; Rom. 16:5). In cities where there were a large number of Christians, several houses were used as meeting places for smaller sections of the larger congregation (Acts 2:46). The church at Colosse met in the house of Philemon (Philem. 2), but this church met in the house of Nymphas. This church was located either in Laodicea or Hierapolis, probably the latter because the former assembly had already been greeted ("the brethren"). Separate church buildings did not become a reality until the third century.

4. The epistles (4:16)

Two epistles are discussed here. *First,* the Epistle to the Colossians ("this epistle") was to be read in two places: at Colosse and at Laodicea. Since only the original manuscript existed, the letter had to be read publicly to the entire congregation.

At the conclusion of his first Thessalonian correspondence, Paul wrote: "I charge you by the Lord that this epistle be read unto all the holy brethren" (I Thess. 5:27). Since the epistles written

---

[12] The critical Greek text reads Nympha (feminine) instead of Nymphas (masculine). The subsequent pronoun is also changed from "his" to "her."

by divinely-approved apostles were inspired and authoritative (II Tim. 3:16; II Peter 1:20–21), they immediately became the basis for faith and practice. All believers thus needed to know about the doctrinal content of their faith and its implications for their behavior. The Book of Revelation contains this blessing: "Blessed is he that readeth, and they that hear the words of this prophecy, and keep those things which are written therein" (Rev. 1:3). There was a single reader, but there were multiple listeners.

The Epistle to the Colossians, although sent to that church, did not become its private possession. The truth of that letter became the doctrinal standard for other churches and believers as well; thus it became necessary to circulate the letters. At this time copies were made so that each church could have at least one.

The public reading of the Old Testament was an essential part of synagogue worship (Luke 4:16–20; Acts 17:2). With this precedent, the reading of the New Testament epistles in the local churches also became a policy as the epistles were written and circulated.

Second, there is a controversy about the identity of "the epistle from Laodicea." Some scholars think it was a letter written by the Laodicean church to Paul, or one written by Paul which has been lost, or the Ephesian letter. The third view seems to be most plausible.[13] Since Tychicus carried the Ephesian letter to that church, it would be logical to assume that the epistle was passed from church to church in the province of Asia. The Book of Revelation was sent to seven churches and was to be read by each, starting with Ephesus and ending with Laodicea (Rev. 1:11). This order followed the sequence of cities on the major road in that region. If the letter to the Ephesians had been circulated in the same fashion, it would have arrived last at Laodicea. Colosse and Laodicea were to exchange the epistles as the process of circulation continued among the churches.

---

[13]This view is held by Herbert M. Carson, *The Epistles of Paul to the Colossians and to Philemon*, p. 101, and by Everett F. Harrison, *Colossians: Christ All-sufficient*, p. 118.

THE BLESSING OF FRIENDS

B. Archippus (4:17)

Five truths about his life can be learned from this verse. *First,* his name means "horse ruler" *(Archippōi).* Paul called Archippus a "fellowsoldier" (Philem. 2). He may have been the natural son of Philemon and Apphia (Philem. 1–2). Quite possibly, he might have been the pastor of the Colossian church in the absence of Epaphras. This church met in the house of Philemon (Philem. 2).

Second, Archippus was responsible to the church. Paul gave instructions to the church to speak to Archippus ("say"). The choice of verb shows that the church was to encourage him, not to compel him.

Third, Archippus was to be watchful over his ministry. The command, earlier translated as "Beware" (2:8), denotes scrutiny and vigilance. It involved evaluation and persistent attention.

Fourth, Archippus possessed "the ministry" *(tēn diakonian).* This noun can be used either of the office of deacon (I Tim. 3:8–13) or the general ministry of preaching. Paul identified himself as a "minister" (1:23) and claimed that Christ had put him into the ministry (I Tim. 1:12). The definite article ("the") points to a specific task which Archippus had to discharge.

Fifth, this spiritual ministry came from the Lord and derived its authority from Him ("which thou hast received in the Lord"). Archippus was ultimately responsible to Christ for his success or failure.

C. Closing Remarks (4:18)

1. Salutation

Paul always personally wrote the closing words of his epistles: "The salutation by the hand of me Paul" (cf. I Cor. 16:21). He used an amanuensis or secretary to compose the major part of a letter because his eyesight apparently was poor (Rom. 16:22; Gal. 4:15). He always signed the epistles so his readers would know they were genuine letters from him (II Thess. 3:17). In one instance, a false teacher forged a letter using the apostle's name and sent it to Thessalonica (II Thess. 2:2). When Paul wrote, he used extremely large letters (plural in the original Greek; Gal. 6:11).

2. Request

Paul asked the Colossians to pray for him: "Remember my bonds." He did not want to be forgotten in prison. When he wrote, the movement of his hand probably caused the chain to clank.

3. Blessing

Paul's closing blessing was direct and simple: "Grace be with you." The heretics elevated legalistic self-effort at the expense of the doctrine of grace. Men are saved by grace alone and they should walk by the principles of grace.

Questions for Discussion

1. What are the qualifications for a church representative? How can these qualities be recognized in a believer?

2. How can Christians overcome their early failures in their spiritual lives? Do churches fail to give believers a second chance?

3. How can believers bring comfort and relief to others? How involved should we be in others' lives?

4. What are the marks of a strong prayer life? Do churches spend enough time in corporate prayer?

5. In what ways can laymen (especially doctors, lawyers, or businessmen) have an effective witness?

6. What is the difference between reading and studying the Bible? What is a good balance?

7. How do believers fail to complete their tasks? How can they break this habit?

Part 2
Philemon

Introduction

I. WRITER

Of the four prison Epistles, this is the only one written directly to an individual. Pauline authorship is self-evident through the repetition of his name (1, 9, 19). The listed associates were with Paul during his Roman confinement (1, 23–24). He identified himself twice as "a prisoner of Jesus Christ" (1, 9) and as the "aged" (9); both of these appellatives would fit into Paul's life history at this time. Its similarity to Colossians (1–2, 23–24; cf. Col. 4:10–17) argues for a simultaneous writing from the same place by the same author.

II. TIME AND PLACE

Onesimus (10), a slave of Philemon who lived in Colosse, had stolen some of his master's goods and fled to Rome (18–19). In the imperial city Onesimus somehow came into contact with Paul, who led the slave into a saving knowledge of Christ during the apostle's captivity (10). For a while Onesimus stayed in Rome and ministered to Paul's material needs, perhaps as a house servant or chef (11, 13). Paul, however, knew that the slave had to be returned to his legal master (13–14). Since Tychicus was returning to the province of Asia with the letters to the Ephesians and Colossians (Eph. 6:21–22; Col. 4:7–8), Paul decided to send Onesimus back to Philemon with his messenger. The letter was thus composed to explain the situation to Philemon and to instruct the master as to how the runaway slave, now a Christian, should be received. This personal letter, then, was written from Rome during Paul's first imprisonment (A.D. 60).

Some current thinkers believe that the book was actually sent to Archippus, the real owner of Onesimus. To them, Philemon was the general overseer of the Christian work in Laodicea, Hierapolis, and Colosse, with his residence in Colosse. Paul sent the letter and the slave first to Philemon, who in turn brought them to Archippus. It was planned that Philemon would exert pressure on Archippus so he would comply with Paul's request. In so doing, these people equate the Epistle to Philemon with the "epistle from Laodicea" (Col. 4:16). Also, the fulfillment of Archippus' ministry would be in the release of Onesimus (Col. 4:17). Although this novel approach appears plausible in places, it has not received acceptance by evangelical scholars. Since Philemon was mentioned first, the book must have been written to him. If it had been written to Archippus, the text would have read "to the church in his house" rather than "your house." Also, the simple explanation of Archippus' ministry is the general ministry (perhaps the pastorate), not a specific task (to set a designated slave free).

III. PURPOSES

In this intimate letter Paul wrote to commend Philemon for his Christian compassion toward the needs of fellow believers (1–7); to effect the forgiveness and restoration of Onesimus by Philemon (8–21); to announce plans of a future visit, based on his hopes of an imminent release (22); and to send greetings from many of Paul's associates who were probably known to Philemon (23–25).

IV. DISTINCTIVE FEATURES

The finest human illustration of the theological concepts of forgiveness and imputation permeates this book. Paul earlier wrote: "And be ye kind one to another, tenderhearted, forgiving one another, even as God for Christ's sake hath forgiven you" (Eph.

4:32). Human forgiveness should reflect divine forgiveness. To the spiritually sensitive, the personages of Paul, Philemon, and Onesimus symbolize respectively Christ, the Father, and the converted sinner. When Paul besought Philemon to receive the slave forever as Paul himself (12, 15, 17), the truth that God accepts believing sinners in the beloved one, Christ, takes on flesh. Paul also wrote: "If he hath wronged thee, or oweth thee ought, put that on mine account . . . I will repay it" (17, 18). This is the language of imputation (cf. II Cor. 5:19–21). The debt of the sinner (sin, guilt, and penalty) was paid by Christ's redemptive death. The person who paid the debt is also the one in whom the believer finds an acceptable standing.

Although the Bible nowhere directly attacks the institution of human slavery, principles for the humane treatment of slaves are found everywhere (Eph. 6:5–9; Col. 3:22—4:1; I Tim. 6:1–2; I Peter 2:18–25). Slaves were to be treated as people, not as property. In this personal letter, however, this is a hint of a principle which would lead a Christian master to release his slaves, especially those who were Christian. Paul wanted Philemon to receive Onesimus "not now as a servant [slave], but above a servant, a brother beloved" (16). He later added: "Having confidence in thy obedience I wrote unto thee, knowing that thou wilt also do more than I say" (21). The words "more than I say" provide the clue. Do they not contain Paul's hope and prayer that Philemon would not only forgive Onesimus, but that he would also release Onesimus from the yoke of human bondage? The principle is clear: If God our heavenly master freed us who were slaves to sin, should we not also release men from human slavery if it is within our power to do so?

12

The Approach to Philemon
Philemon 1–9

One of the Beatitudes states: "Blessed are the peacemakers; for they shall be called the children of God" (Matt. 5:9). In his attempt to effect a reconciliation of loving brotherhood between Philemon and Onesimus, Paul personified that biblical principle. The difficulty behind his task was real and significant, caused by the geographical barrier and the cultural disparity. God, however, used Paul's diplomatic epistle to eliminate both problems.

I. GREETINGS (1–3)

This brief letter contains the distinctive marks of a Pauline epistle: name, position, associate, readers, and blessing.

A. Author (1a)

All of Paul's letters begin with the mention of his name. His life was discussed earlier (Col. 1:1).

1. His position

Paul identified himself in two ways. *First,* he was a "prisoner." This is the only epistle which has this opening description. This title would no doubt appeal to Philemon's sentiment and would fit in with Paul's approach to his friend. He planned to make a request rather than to issue a command.

Second, Paul was a prisoner "of Jesus Christ." He was no ordinary prisoner. This fact soon became evident to those authorities who were involved in his case. Elsewhere he wrote: "So that my bonds in Christ are manifest in all the palace, and in all other places" (Phil. 1:13). It was soon known that the apostle was before the Roman court because he was a Christian, not because he had committed a civil crime. Paul himself knew that he was there by the will of God. The government officials may have thought that he was their prisoner, but he recognized that he really was "the prisoner of the Lord" (Eph. 4:1). He was a spiritual, heaven-sent "ambassador in bonds" (Eph. 6:20). Thus, the apostle was in Rome as a witness, not as a defendant. He asked his friends to pray for this unique opportunity of outreach (Eph. 6:19–20; Col. 4:3–4).

His associate

Timothy, whose life was also discussed earlier, was with Paul at Rome. He is called, literally, "the brother" (*ho adelphos;* cf. Col. 1:1). The term comes from two Greek words (*apo* and *delphus*) which mean "from the same womb." Timothy was a brother not only to Paul, but also to Philemon. All three men had been born of God and therefore shared in the same divine nature. The relationship that Timothy sustained to the other two was the same relationship that Paul wanted Philemon to manifest toward Onesimus (16). This descriptive title was used therefore with deliberate intent.

B. Recipients (1b–2)

Lightfoot said that "the letter introduces us to an ordinary household in a small town in Phrygia. Four members of it are mentioned by name, the father, the mother, the son, and the slave."[1]

1. Philemon (1b)

As the head of the household, Philemon is naturally addressed first. This is the only New Testament book in which his name is

[1] J. B. Lightfoot, *St. Paul's Epistles to the Colossians and to Philemon,* p. 303.

found. He knew Paul personally and was without doubt converted through the apostle's ministry, possibly during Paul's lengthy stay at Ephesus (19; cf. Acts 19). Elsewhere in the epistle, Paul directly addresses him as "brother" (7, 20).

Philemon is described here in two ways. *First,* his relationship to Paul and Timothy was as "our dearly beloved." They all shared a reciprocal love. This affectionate word is later used of Onesimus (16). Paul wanted Philemon to love his slave in the same way that the apostle loved Philemon.

Second, Philemon's position was that of "fellowlabourer." Paul and Philemon were joint workers in the cause of Christ. In the past they perhaps worked together in Ephesus or some other city in Asia; however, this may just be a general statement. As Paul labored in Rome and Philemon labored in Colosse, they became fellow laborers for the glory of the Savior.

2. *Apphia (2a)*

Lightfoot believes it is a "safe inference" to say that Apphia was Philemon's wife.[2] This is the only place that her name appears in the New Testament.

Apphia also was "beloved" *(tēi agapētēi).*[3] She was a beloved sister to Paul in the family of God. The instructions given to Philemon about the proper treatment of Onesimus would likewise apply to her treatment of Onesimus.

3. *Archippus (2b)*

His name means "horse ruler." If one accepts that Apphia was Philemon's wife, then it logically follows that Archippus was their son. His name appears twice in the New Testament (2; Col. 4:17). He was in the gospel ministry in Colosse or Laodicea, probably the latter. Since the two cities were near each other, Lightfoot concluded: "Archippus must have been in constant communication with his parents, who lived there; and it was therefore quite natural that, writing to the father and mother, St. Paul should

[2] *Ibid.,* p. 306.
[3] The critical Greek text substitutes "sister" for "beloved."

mention the son's name also in the opening address, though he was not on the spot."[4]

Paul identified Archippus as "our fellowsoldier." This complementary term is used elsewhere only of Epaphroditus (Phil. 2:25). This general title describes their common struggle as good soldiers of Jesus Christ (II Tim. 2:3). They became acquainted at Ephesus, and may also have been spiritual comrades in arms there.

4. The local church (2c)

The word "church" *(ekklēsiā)* is formed from two words which mean "to call out from." A church, therefore, is a called-out group of believers. The term can refer to the universal church, that group of believers which has been divinely called out of a sinful world into Christ in this present age between the descent of the Holy Spirit and the translation of the church (Matt. 16:18; Eph. 1:22–23). Usually, the term refers to the local church, the group of believers assembled together in one place for the worship of God and the observance of Christ's ordinances and commands. This latter usage is intended here.

This assembly met in the house of Philemon ("thy"). This was common. Other "house churches" are mentioned elsewhere (Rom. 16:5; I Cor. 16:19; Col. 4:15). Private church buildings were constructed much later in the history of the church. Most believers were poor freemen or slaves. Therefore they probably did not own property—certainly not buildings that could accommodate a large gathering. Since Philemon did own such a house, he must have been both wealthy and hospitable. Such kindness now needed to be demonstrated toward Onesimus.

C. Blessing (3)

1. Its content

First, "grace" *(charis)* is divine favor without regard to merit or repayment. It does not mean that the recipient of the grace is unworthy, only that the basis of giving is without regard to human

---

[4] Lightfoot, *St. Paul's Epistles,* p. 309.

merit. Every blessing of life, whether physical or spiritual, is a direct result of divine grace. This reference is to that grace which God gives every day to sustain His own (John 1:16).

Second, "peace" (eirēnē) appears next, and rightly so. Unless there is a manifestation of grace, there can be no peace. When believers are regenerated, they have positional peace before God (Rom. 5:1). The reference here is to that practical peace which protects the child of God from nervous and mental disorders (Phil. 4:7). The believer can enjoy this provision every day if he claims it by faith.

2. Its recipients

The change from the singular in verse 2 (sou) to the plural "you" (humin) shows that Paul wanted Philemon, Apphia, Archippus, and the entire church to share in the blessing from God. It was not intended for just one person, Philemon, but for all.

3. Its source

There is a double source of the blessing.[5] First, it originates from "God our Father." He is God; He is the Father; and believers are related to Him ("our"). He is not the Father of unsaved humanity, but He becomes the Father of a repentant sinner at the time of his conversion. He is not the Father of a believer in the same sense as the Father-Son relationship within the trinitarian oneness of the divine Being. The former begins in time; the latter has always existed.

Second, the blessing also stems from "the Lord Jesus Christ." He who is one with the Father gives to the Christian daily grace and peace as the believer permits the gracious Prince of Peace to live His life through him.

II. THANKSGIVING (4–7)

Paul thanked God for people as well as for things. His thanksgiving was both personal and constant ("I thank"),[6] but later he

---

[5] Indicated by the single preposition "from" (apo) and a double object.

[6] Present active indicative, first person singular.

expressed joy for both Timothy and himself ("we have," 7). The concept of thanksgiving is derived from two words: "well" *(eu)* and "grace" *(charis)*. When God graciously gives favors to a believer, the Christian does well to respond with thanks.

A. Its Fact (4)

1. Its object

Every good and perfect gift descends from God (James 1:17); therefore, thanks should ultimately be given to Him. As a believer-priest, Paul was able to communicate with God by offering the sacrifices of praise and thanksgiving (Heb. 13:15). The personal pronoun "my" shows the intimacy of relationship between the Christian and his creator.

2. Its time

The adverb "always" *(pantote)* grammatically can modify either the main verb ("thank") or the following participle ("making").[7] Paul did not remember Philemon every time he prayed, but when the apostle did mention his friend's name, he always gave thanks for the master of Onesimus.

3. Its occasion

The occasion for thanksgiving is seen in the participial phrase ("making mention of thee in my prayers"). Paul believed in both the sovereign purposes of God and the personal responsibility of private prayer. Philemon probably was thrilled and impressed to read that the busy apostle took time to pray for him and even to give thanks for him. Paul was an intercessor. He believed that God would work in the lives of others as a direct result of his concern.

B. Its Cause (5)

Paul heard a report which caused him to give thanks.[8] How did

[7] Both Kent and Robertson relate it to the former.
[8] Causal usage of the participle ("hearing").

he receive this information? Since Epaphras told about the faith and love of the Colossian believers (Col. 1:4, 8), it is very likely that he informed Paul about the spiritual outreach of Philemon. Two areas of special commendation formed the basis for the apostle's gratitude.

1. The love of Philemon

The love of Philemon ("thy love") is isolated here for special mention. Although Apphia and Archippus are not specifically included in this reference, they undoubtedly assisted Philemon in his gracious acts of hospitality. His love *(agapēn)* was a manifestation of the fruit of the Spirit (Gal. 5:22). This love is the highest type, based on a recognition of value or worth in the object.

Philemon's love was directed "toward all saints." He saw value in all of the saints because both they and he were members of the family of God. Believers "are taught of God to love one another" (I Thess. 4:9), an evidence of genuine salvation (I John 3:14). Philemon was not partial; he manifested his love to *all* the saints: the men and the women; the Jews and the Gentiles; and the freemen and the slaves. Now Paul wanted Philemon to include one more believer in that group, namely, Onesimus.

2. The faith of Philemon

Paul did not refer to Philemon's initial saving faith, but rather to his daily, practical faith which the Christian should exercise as he walks by faith.[9] This faith was Philemon's daily possession ("thou hast").[10] Faith is simply that conviction of heart and mind which leads a person to commit himself to Christ completely, first for salvation, then for daily spiritual sustenance.

Faith must have an object. The value of faith depends on the value of the object. Philemon's faith was true and valid because it was directed "toward the Lord Jesus," the true and faithful one.

There is a slight grammatical problem in this verse. What is the relationship of the two nouns ("love" and "faith") to the two

---

[9] This faith is definite, indicated by the article *(tēn pistin)*.

[10] Present active indicative: *echeis*.

prepositional phrases? Lightfoot observed: "The logical order is violated, and the clauses are inverted in the second part of the sentence, thus producing an example of the figure called chiasm."[11] Chiasm follows the literary procedure of 1–4:2–3. The first (love) and fourth (saints) concepts go together, whereas the second (faith) and third (Lord) are joined. Elsewhere, love is manward and faith is Godward (Eph. 1:15; Col. 1:4) If "faith" means "faithfulness" in this context, then love and faithfulness could have been extended to both the Lord and the saints.

C. Its Purpose (6)

The connective "that" *(hopōs)* shows the purpose for the intercessory prayer of thanksgiving (4).

1. Effective fellowship

Paul prayed "that the communication of thy faith may become effectual." The word "communication" *(koinōnia)* normally is translated as "fellowship" (I John 1:3, 6–7). It is that which is shared, that which is commonly possessed. The fellowship of Philemon's faith may simply point to the common life which he shared with other believers, but it seems to imply something more in this context. In the past, Philemon had shared his material goods with needy Christians (7). He brought physical relief through his acts of brotherly love.

Now, Paul wanted Philemon to share the practical expression of his faith in a new experience. He wanted Philemon's faith to "become effectual" through the kind reception of Onesimus and the subsequent release of the Christian slave.

2. Total knowledge

The sphere of effective fellowship is in "the acknowledging of every good thing which is in you in Christ Jesus."[12] The reading of this epistle would give Philemon such understanding. His acts

---

[11] Lightfoot, *St. Paul's Epistles*, p. 334.
[12] The preposition "by" is actually "in" *(en)*.

of Christian charity were to find total expression in all human situations involving members of the family of God ("every good thing").

This goodness *(agathou)*, which corresponded to the character of God, was found only in believers ("in you").[13] It was in Philemon and his family, and it dwelled within Paul and his associate.

Carson wrote: "But at once [Paul] corrects any idea that such blessings are for the believer's personal enjoyment. He speaks rather in terms of blessings which have Christ as their goal."[14] All displays of brotherly love must literally be done "unto *[eis]* Christ Jesus," for His honor and glory; otherwise, they are mere humanistic manifestations of philanthropy. Christ said to believers who fed and clothed the hungry and the naked: "Inasmuch as ye have done it unto one of the least of these my brethren, ye have done it unto me" (Matt. 25:40). That principle applies to all interpersonal relationships within the family of God.

D. Its Reason (7)

The explanatory connective "for" *(gar)* goes back to the main verb ("I thank"). Paul gave thanks, for he had much joy and comfort.

1. Presence of joy and comfort

Paul and Timothy were both pleased by the kindness of Philemon ("we have").[15] It brought them "joy and consolation." The former emotion looks back at what had been done, and the latter provides encouragement in the present and for the future. Paul received comfort in his own imprisonment, and the generosity of Philemon encouraged the apostle to send this epistle of intercession for Onesimus. In fact, he literally had "much" *(pollēn)* emotional strength.

The basis of this joy and comfort was the love of Philemon ("in

[13] The critical Greek text has "in us."

[14] Herbert M. Carson, *The Epistles of Paul to the Colossians and to Philemon,* p. 106.

[15] The critical Greek text has *eschon* ("I had") rather than *echomen* ("we have"). Regardless, Timothy shared in Paul's joy.

thy love"). Literally, it reads "upon *(epi)* your love." Paul heard about this love from the Colossian representative (5).

2. Relief of the saints

The connective "because" *(hoti)* gives the cause for this joy and comfort. Paul rejoiced "because the bowels of the saints are refreshed." The unusual descriptive term "bowels" *(splagchna)* refers to the deep, inner emotional needs of a person (see the discussion about Colossians 3:12b in chapter 9). Paul thanked God because the physical and emotional needs of his fellow believers had been satisfied. The verb stresses both the initial act of hospitality and the subsequent state of personal satisfaction.[16] Elsewhere, Paul advised: "As we have therefore opportunity, let us do good unto all men, especially unto them who are of the household of faith" (Gal. 6:10). A spiritual Christian will be involved in "distributing to the necessity of saints; given to hospitality" (Rom. 12:13). Believers must be altruistic and humanitarian in their living, or else their profession of faith will be vain (James 2:14–17).

Paul's joy took an added significance because the saints had been refreshed through his friend Philemon ("by thee, brother"). Philemon was the agent *(dia)* through whom God met the needs of His children. God works in and through the compassionate concern of involved believers to provide food, clothing, and shelter for His own (Matt. 6:25–34). It is difficult to have anxiety in the presence of loving brothers and sisters.

III. APPEAL (8–9)

The first seven verses were introductory. They provided the framework for the forthcoming discussion about Onesimus. Specifically, the real purpose for sending the personal epistle becomes apparent at verse 8. Paul is now about to appeal to Philemon to forgive and to receive the converted runaway slave as a spiritual brother.

The inferential conjunction "wherefore" *(dio)* introduces this

---

[16] Perfect passive indicative: *anapepautai*.

section. Since Philemon had manifested past kindness toward all other saints, Paul inferred that his friend would show equal grace to a new brother, Onesimus.

How should the appeal be made? Paul had two choices. With an open heart, he disclosed to Philemon the basis of appeal which he rejected, and the one which he followed.

A. Authority (8)

1. Paul had authority over Philemon

Paul's authority was only in the spiritual realm ("in Christ"), in the sphere that pertained to Christ and to His gospel, because that was the domain to which he had been called. This was not civil or social authority; rather, it was ecclesiastical. Christ commissioned Paul to become an apostle (I Cor. 9:1–2; 15:8–10; Gal. 1:1). Apostles had primary, general authority over all churches and believers (I Cor. 12:28; Eph. 4:11). They laid the foundation for the church in their oral and written exposition of the significance of Christ's redemptive work (Eph. 2:20).

Such authority gave Paul literally "much boldness" (pollēn parrēsian). This phrase denotes a total freedom to speak dogmatically under the supervision of the Holy Spirit. Only apostles and their officially designated representatives could demand obedience for their directives to the churches (I Cor. 4:16–21; II Thess. 3:14).

2. Paul could command Philemon

The apostle had the right "to enjoin thee [Philemon] that which is convenient." If he had chosen to do so, Paul could have forced Philemon to comply with the former's wishes. In that situation, Paul could have commanded the Colossian assembly to discipline Philemon if the latter had refused to obey. In fact, forgiveness is not optional; it is obligatory to each believer (Col. 3:12–13).

B. Love (9)

Paul chose "rather" (mallon) to exhort Philemon as friend to friend, brother to brother, not as an apostle to a church member. The closeness of their relationship is further seen in his usage of the verb "beseech" (*parakalō*) rather than a direct imperative.[17]

1. Appeal out of love

Paul did not command Philemon "for love's sake." Paul dearly loved his spiritual brother (1,7), and loved ones do not command each other. The usage of the definite article ("the love") shows that this was the apostle's specific love for Philemon, not a general love for all men.

2. Appeal out of position

Paul identified himself to the church at Colosse as an apostle (Col. 1:1), but he did not mention that high office to Philemon. He approached his friend on the basis of two positions.

First, he was "Paul the aged." There is a slight textual problem here. Some Greek manuscripts read "aged" (*presbutēs*) while others contain the word "ambassador" (*presbeutēs*). Paul, of course, was both. Since ambassadors were usually mature, experienced men, the concepts of age and diplomacy go together. Elsewhere, he described himself as "an ambassador in bonds" (Eph. 6:20). As an ambassador for Christ, he was committed to the ministry of reconciliation (II Cor. 5:20). The purpose behind this very epistle was to bring Philemon and Onesimus together in a new loving relationship. An ambassador, of course, is one who blends authority with gracious humility and courtesy. Such tact marked Paul's approach.

Second, he was "also a prisoner of Jesus Christ." This second mention of his imprisonment served to invoke sympathy within Philemon (1). How could the benevolent Philemon refuse any request from his close friend who was in Rome for the cause of Christ?

Questions for Discussion

1. How many of your friends and relatives would you describe

---

[17] The verb is related to the noun "consolation" (*paraklēsin*, 7).

as "beloved"? How does a believer gain such an intimate relationship with another?

2. How can whole families work together in the cause of Christ? How can the charge of nepotism be avoided?

3. Should believers meet in houses today? What advantages or disadvantages are there in meeting in private homes? in church buildings?

4. In what ways can believers manifest hospitality? to the unsaved? to strangers? to church members?

5. Do Christians restrict their generosity to a select group of friends? to members of their own race?

6. What types of social programs should churches support? How much time and money should be invested in them?

7. When should parents deal with their children out of mere authority? out of love? out of both?

13

The Appeal to Philemon
Philemon 10–25

The opening words, "I beseech thee," begin the formal appeal. Paul repeated the verb for emphasis and for effect. He made it clear that he was not issuing a command.

I. HIS REQUEST (10–20)

The personal character of the epistle becomes especially evident in this section. In the English text, Paul frequently refers to himself: "I" (eight times); "me" (seven); "my" or "mine" (six); and "myself" (once). Such an intimate request must have had an impact on the heart of Philemon.

A. Object of Request (10–14)

The preposition "for" (*peri*) indicates the person for whom Paul is making request. Eight statements describe him.

1. He was Paul's child (10a)

Who can resist an appeal when it concerns a child? For example, foreign orphanages often make financial requests and show pictures of starving and naked children. These requests appeal to such human compassion.

The slave was literally the "child" (*teknou*) of Paul, rather than his son. Paul used the emphatic possessive adjective ("my") to stress the spiritual father-child relationship which now existed between him and Onesimus *(tou emou teknou)*. The grace of God is also magnified here by the fact that a free Jew claims to be the spiritual father of a Gentile slave.

2. He was Onesimus (10b)

Philemon, his family, and the Colossian church must have been surprised when Onesimus reappeared along with Tychicus and the two epistles. They probably thought that he was gone forever, but now he had come back into their lives.

Onesimus' name literally means "profitable." It is based on the noun "profit" *(onēsis)* and the verb "to profit" *(oninēmi)*. In the verse, the name actually appears last, after the statement of birth. Paul described the relationship before he gave the name of the new spiritual child.

3. He was born in Paul's bonds (10c)

Although repentant sinners are born of God, receive His nature, and are therefore the children of God (John 1:12–13), yet in some sense it can still be said that one Christian gives spiritual birth to another. Paul recognized this truth by stating his active participation in the evangelistic birth process ("whom I have begotten in my bonds"). He witnessed to Onesimus and led him into a saving experience with Christ; therefore, he had begotten the slave. Elsewhere, Paul described this same human involvement in bringing people into the family of God: ". . . for in Christ Jesus I have begotten you through the gospel" (I Cor. 4:15). God and man labor together at the moment of the new birth; both need each other. Paul explained his physical and emotional involvement with these maternal words: "My little children, of whom I travail in birth again until Christ be formed in you" (Gal. 4:19).

The conversion of Onesimus occurred during Paul's imprisonment at Rome ("in my bonds"). In his other confinements, the apostle had led the Philippian jailor and possibly some other prisoners to Christ (Acts 16:25–34).

4. He was once unprofitable (11a)

Three features are indicated. *First*, Onesimus was "unprofitable" *(achrēston)*. This adjective is derived from a verb which means "not to use" *(a* and *chraomai)*. He thus was a useless slave, one who failed to do his assigned tasks and who eventually cheated his master and fled.

Second, this profitless life was "in time past" *(pote)*, the period of his unsaved life when he served Philemon.

Third, Onesimus was useless to Philemon ("to thee"). As the human owner, Philemon became frustrated over the indolence of Onesimus.

5. *He was now profitable (11b)*

Three aspects of the radical change are stated. *First*, the sharp contrast between the past and the present can be seen in the two adverbs: "once" *(pote)* . . . "but now" *(nuni de)*. The conversion of Onesimus ended one phase of his life and started the next.

Second, Onesimus was "profitable" *(euchrēston)*. He not only was of use now, but he was of good *(eu)* use. Since he became saved, his life took on new meaning and motivation. He personified the principles which should mark the life of a Christian slave (Col. 3:22–25).

Third, Onesimus was profitable now to both Philemon and Paul. Although Philemon had known nothing about his slave's conversion and service at Rome, the order of the words, "to thee and to me," indicates that the usefulness of Onesimus to Philemon had already started.

6. *He was sent back (12a)*

At the time Paul commissioned Tychicus with the two epistles (Colossians and Philemon), he also sent Onesimus. Ellis commented: "The verb translated 'sent back' (ASV) can have the technical judicial meaning of 'to refer a case,' i.e., to allow Philemon himself to judge in the matter of Onesimus' freedom (cf. Luke 23:7, 11; Acts 25:21)."[1] Within that culture, Paul had to send a runaway slave back to his master. In addition, as a new believer, Onesimus needed to ask forgiveness and to make restitution for

---

[1] Earle Ellis, "Philemon," *The Wycliffe Bible Commentary*, p. 1398.

past wrongs. Like the prodigal son, he needed to confess before Philemon: "I have sinned against heaven, and before thee" (Luke 15:18).

7. He was Paul's bowels (12b)

Paul called Onesimus "mine own bowels" (ta ema splagchna). Earlier, Philemon had been commended for refreshing "the bowels of the saints" (7). Now, Paul wanted his friend to give the same generous reception to the converted slave. The apostle thus equated himself and his inner needs with Onesimus. The treatment of the slave in effect would manifest the treatment of the apostle, and vice versa.

The command was personal, direct, and decisive: ". . . thou therefore receive him."[2] Actually, the pronoun "you" (su) appears at the beginning of the statement, and the imperative (proslabou) is placed last.

8. He was a minister (13–14)

Onesimus profitably "ministered" in Rome after his conversion. This information probably shocked Philemon and his family. At this point, Paul shared his plans and feelings in three definitive statements. First, he wanted to keep Onesimus in Rome ("whom I would have retained with me"). A close working relationship developed between the two; thus, the apostle did not want him to leave. He was willing (eboulomēn) to retain Onesimus, but he could not force his desire on an unwilling Philemon.

Second, Paul wanted Onesimus to serve as the representative of Philemon in Rome ("in thy stead"). Epaphras represented the Colossians, Epaphroditus represented the Philippians, and Onesimus could do the same for Philemon. Paul disclosed that the converted slave "might have ministered unto [him]." The verb (diakonēi) refers to a general ministry, not to the technical service of a church deacon. In what sense could Onesimus minister to Paul? He could work as a domestic servant in the apostle's hired house (Acts 28:30), pray, witness, and assist the Roman church. There is a tradition, stemming from the letter of Ignatius to the Ephe-

---

[2]The command is not found in the critical Greek text.

sians, that Onesimus later became a minister and subsequently the bishop of the Ephesian church.[3] Since Paul was imprisoned ("in the bonds of the gospel"), Onesimus could have carried out strategic errands for the apostle.

Third, Paul wanted Philemon to make a voluntary decision about the future of Onesimus (14). The decision to retain Onesimus was not Paul's to make. Onesimus belonged to Philemon. Paul had to inform Philemon before he proceeded any further in his plans for Onesimus ("But without thy mind would I do nothing"). The noun "mind" *(gnōmēs)* stresses the concept of knowledge; by extension, it implies an informed, knowledgeable intellect. Philemon needed to have all the facts, and the only way for that to happen was to send Onesimus back.

The question centered around Philemon's "benefit," literally his "good" *(to agathon sou).* Earlier, Paul expressed his concern over an effective fellowship "by the acknowledging of every good thing which is in you" (6). Philemon's prior hospitality had been offered freely out of love; thus, if he manifested goodness to Onesimus, it could not stem from a forced compliance to the apostle's desire. It could not be "of necessity" *(kata anagkēn);* otherwise he would forfeit the divine blessing for his good deed. Rather, it had to be done "willingly" *(kata ekousion).* The strong contrast between the standard of legalism and that of grace can be seen in the negative-positive comparison and the presence of the strong adversative "but" *(alla).* In giving money, a believer must do so "not grudgingly, or of necessity: for God loveth a cheerful giver" (II Cor. 9:7). Such principles should also guide in the giving of forgiveness and in the freeing of slaves. Paul thus transferred the future of Onesimus from his will to the mind and will of Philemon.

B. Background of Request (15–16)

The connective "for" *(gar)* joins this section to the preceding one. It introduces the reason for Onesimus' flight, his conversion, and his return to Philemon.

---

[3] Ellis, "Philemon," p. 1398.

STAND PERFECT IN WISDOM

1. The separation (15a)

Why did Onesimus run away? Paul suggested an explanation ("perhaps"). His disobedient separation was within God's permissive will and was used by God to produce the conversion of Onesimus. What the slave did was wrong, but God can overrule wrong and use it to accomplish His ultimate purpose (Ps. 76:10; Rom. 8:28). In his testimony to the sovereign, providential direction of God, Joseph remarked to his fearful brothers: "But as for you, ye thought evil against me; but God meant it unto good, to bring to pass, as it is this day, to save much people alive" (Gen. 50:20).

The verb "departed" *(echōristhē)* suggests that the slave was separated from Philemon by the will of God.[4] Onesimus bore the moral responsibility for his defection, but God actively was working out His will to get the slave to Rome and into direct contact with the apostle.

The separation was both brief and temporary ("for a season"). Literally, it reads "for an hour" *(pros hōran)*.

2. The reception (15b–16)

The purpose for the separation is indicated in the clause introduced by "that" *(hina)*. The separation has led to a reception. Perhaps, if there had been no separation, there would have been no reception. Since God has ordained both the end and the means to that end, His sovereign purpose must be recognized within human circumstances.

Three characteristics of the reception are delineated. *First*, Philemon would receive Onesimus "for ever." What is an hour compared to eternity? Temporary separation and service is so insignificant in relation to eternal fellowship and brotherhood. The verb "receive" *(apecheis)* conveys the ideas of restitution and completeness. It means "to have back, to have in return, to have the full." Philemon lost an unregenerate slave temporarily, but he received in return an eternal brother. In a sense, the conversion

---

[4] Aorist passive indicative.

and return of Onesimus was a divine payment for the loss of his past services.

Second, Philemon should receive Onesimus "not now as a servant." His treatment of Onesimus could no longer be the same, now that conversion had taken place. The little comparative word "as" *(hōs)* is critical here. Onesimus was still a slave even though he was saved; however, Philemon could no longer view him as a mere slave ("but above a servant").

Third, Philemon should receive Onesimus as a spiritual brother. The slave was now a "brother," a brother to Paul, Timothy, and even to Philemon. Some brotherly relationships, however, lack personal warmth; thus, Paul wanted Philemon to esteem Onesimus as a "beloved" brother in the same sense that the apostle loved Philemon (1). Paul regarded the master and the slave in the same way. With God and the apostle, there was no respect of persons or social status.

Paul's relationship to Onesimus was close because he led the slave to Christ ("specially to me"). Philemon, however, had known Onesimus longer ("but how much more unto thee"). The brotherly attachment had to be manifested in both the human and spiritual realms ("both in the flesh and in the Lord"). There may be a hint here that Onesimus and Philemon were blood relatives, perhaps even natural brothers. That speculation might explain the flight and the delicate nature of the return.

C. Nature of Request (17–20)

The request to receive Onesimus was given earlier (12). In this section of the personal letter, Paul pressed the issue with a series of three imperatives. Together, they constitute the essence of his appeal.

1. Receive him as me (17)

The basis of this request is found within the conditional clause, "if thou count me therefore a partner." The noun "partner" *(koinōnon)* is related to the word "communication" *(koinōnia;* 6). Paul and Philemon were partners, men who had shared many experiences together, men who were bound by a common reciprocal love, men who shared the same spiritual motivation, and men who possessed a common salvation in Christ. The condition did not express doubt about this relationship; rather, Paul affirmed in it that Philemon did esteem the apostle as a partner.[5]

The appeal itself illustrates the principle of substitution: ". . . receive him as me." Since Philemon would receive Paul as a "brother beloved," then the master would have to welcome the slave in the same way.

This human relationship provides an excellent illustration of the divine program of salvation. By analogy, Philemon represents God the Father, Paul symbolizes Jesus Christ, and Onesimus reflects the repentant sinner. The believer is "accepted in the beloved" Son of God (Eph. 1:6). In essence, Christ says to the Father: "Receive the believing sinner as me."

2. Put that on mine account (18–19)

The basis of this appeal is found within the conditional clause, "if he hath wronged thee, or oweth thee ought."[6] In fact, Onesimus had done both. The first verb "wronged" *(ēdikēse)* deals with a legal injustice (cf. Matt. 20:13; Acts 25:10; I Cor. 6:7–8). In his counsel to Christian slaves and masters, Paul wrote: "But he that doeth wrong shall receive for the wrong which he hath done: and there is no respect of persons" (Col. 3:25). In his unsaved life, Onesimus had violated laws governing slavehood. The second verb, "oweth," implies financial loss through theft. In order to finance his flight, Onesimus probably had stolen money or valuable property which could be converted into cash. That money was depleted by this time. A Christian slave, on the other hand, should be marked by "not purloining, but shewing all good fidelity" (Titus 2:10).

The nature of the appeal is in the directive: "Put that on mine account." This imperative *(ellogei)* is a technical, business term. Paul wanted to assume the debt. It reflected the attitude of the good Samaritan who told the innkeeper: "Take care of him [the

---

[5] It is a first-class condition, using *ei* ("if") with the indicative *(echeis)*.

[6] It is a first-class condition, using *ei* ("if") with two indicative verbs: "wronged" *(ēdikēse)* and "oweth" *(opheilei)*.

pilgrim]; and whatsoever thou spendest more, when I come again, I will repay thee" (Luke 10:35). In such a situation, there must be implicit trust in the person's word and his ability to pay. In the spiritual analogy, it illustrates perfectly the doctrine of judicial imputation: "For he hath made him to be sin for us, who knew no sin; that we might be made the righteousness of God in him" (II Cor. 5:21). God the Father put the wrong and moral debt of the sinful world to the account of Christ; thus the Savior paid the penalty for the sin of the unjust (I Peter 3:18).

The guarantee of payment is contained in two statements: the fact and the promise (19). At this point, Paul may have taken the pen from his amanuensis and finished the writing of the epistle. The unique Pauline script was his signature affixed to the note of indebtedness (Gal. 6:11). Since the apostle had poor eyesight, Philemon must have been emotionally moved when he saw the guarantee written by Paul's own hand.

The promise of future payment was given in spite of the fact that Paul had little money in his possession. In this particular imprisonment, he was thankful for the financial support of others through direct gifts and voluntary labor (Phil. 2:30; 4:14–18). Since repentance involves restitution, Paul offered to make the loss good because he knew that Onesimus had no funds.

Some debts, however, are never recalled; they are either forgotten or canceled. Paul now reminded Philemon of the latter's debt to the apostle ("albeit I do not say to thee how thou owest unto me even thine own self besides"). What was this debt which had never been paid by Philemon? It is possible that Paul had purchased Philemon's freedom from slavery after the latter had become a Christian; however, there is no indication that the wealthy, generous Philemon had ever been a slave. It is more plausible to believe that Paul led Philemon to Christ. Philemon thus owed his salvation and subsequent happiness to the instrumentality of the apostle. To be delivered from the debt of sin and hell is so much greater than to be released from a financial obligation.

3. Refresh me (20)

The basis of this appeal is contained within the heartfelt wish of the apostle ("Yea, brother, let me have joy of thee in the Lord").[7] Ultimately, joy comes from proper relationships between people, not from the possession of things. For believers, however, joy must be heightened by truth and spiritual guidelines ("in the Lord"). Believers are to encourage and edify each other. Paul desired that Philemon might minister to him through the proper treatment of Onesimus.

The nature of the appeal is direct: "Refresh my bowels in the Lord." Paul earlier identified Onesimus as his "bowels" (12). Since Philemon had been commended for refreshing the "bowels of the saints" (7), he now is charged to meet the needs of one more saint. He must not be a respecter of persons; he must treat all believers alike, including Onesimus.

II. HIS CONFIDENCE (21–22)

As the epistle drew to an end, Paul expressed confidence ("having confidence") about two things.

A. In Philemon's Obedience (21)

1. To do what Paul requested

Paul had confidence in Philemon's "obedience" because the apostle knew the character of his distant friend. Philemon obeyed the will of God and manifested that submission through his love and faith (5). Such general obedience now had to be applied to the specific request of Paul. The apostle knew that his friend would obey all of the previous directives both in the letter and in the spirit.

Such confidence caused Paul to write this epistle. If the apostle would have had any doubt about the willingness of Philemon to comply, he would have retained Onesimus in Rome until his own release and return to Colosse (22).

2. To do more than what Paul requested

Since Paul knew Philemon, he had confidence that his friend

[7] The optative verb (onaimēn) expresses a wish.

would go beyond the minimum details of the request: ". . . knowing that thou wilt also do more than I say." How could he do "more"? Philemon could cancel any debt that he held against Onesimus; he could send Onesimus back to Paul in order that the slave might minister to the apostle (13); or he could give Onesimus his freedom. The third option would give Onesimus the choice to remain in Colosse or to rejoin Paul in Rome. The third option fits most closely with the biblical principle to forgive even as one has been forgiven by Christ (Eph. 4:32; Col. 3:13). Paul nowhere charged Philemon to set Onesimus free, but this last statement contains a hint toward that end.

B. In His Release (22)

1. Prepare lodging for me

Paul expected to visit Colosse and Philemon in the future, so he asked his friend to make preparations for his visit. Because of Philemon's past hospitality to others, the apostle knew that there would be a room for him.

2. Reason for release

The explanatory conjunction "for" (gar) gives the reason behind Paul's belief in an imminent release from his Roman imprisonment. Although Caesar would grant the actual political acquittal, Paul knew that God would set him free as an answer to the prayers of many Christians ("through your prayers"; Phil. 1:19). The sovereignty of God and the responsibility of believers, as seen in prayer, complement each other. In fact, Paul looked on his release and return as a gracious gift from God to Philemon and his family.[8]

III. CLOSING REMARKS (23–25)

A. Greetings (23–24)

Five associates wanted to greet Philemon personally ("There sa-

[8]The words "your" (humōn) and "you" (humin) are both plural.

lute thee"). These five were all mentioned in the closing section of the Colossian epistle (Col. 4:10–14).

Epaphras, a member of the Colossian church, apparently had been imprisoned also for the cause of Christ ("my fellowprisoner in Christ Jesus"). His confinement necessitated sending Tychicus with the two letters (Col. 4:7–8).

The four others were still free and were designated as his "fellowlabourers."

B. Benediction (25)

This typical Pauline benediction, with its emphasis on divine grace, was extended to Philemon, his family, and the entire church (1–2). The possessive pronoun "your" (humōn) is plural, not singular. Paul wanted them to have a corporate oneness within their assembly and in their treatment of Onesimus.

Questions for Discussion

1. In what places and circumstances were people saved in biblical days? How do those circumstances correspond to modern evangelistic efforts?

2. How can believers prove to be profitable to others? unprofitable?

3. What different types of ministry are available today? How can believers prepare for these various services?

4. In what ways can a believer force someone to do something out of necessity, rather than willingly? How can this pressure be resisted?

5. How can wrong ultimately end in good? How does the plan of God incorporate the sinfulness of man?

6. How can believers forgive as they have been forgiven by Christ? Is any sin beyond forgiveness?

7. Why should believers pray? How does God bless the prayers of dedicated saints?

Selected Bibliography

Carson, Herbert M. *The Epistles of Paul to the Colossians and to Philemon*. Grand Rapids: Wm. B. Eerdmans Publishing Co., 1977.

Gaebelein, Frank E. *Philemon: the Gospel of Emancipation*. Neptune, NJ: Loizeaux Brothers, 1960.

Harrison, Everett F. *Colossians: Christ All-sufficient*. Chicago: Moody Press, 1971.

Hendriksen, William. *New Testament Commentary: Exposition of Colossians and Philemon*. Grand Rapids: Baker Book House, 1964.

Ironside, H. A. *Lectures on the Epistle to the Colossians*. Neptune, NJ: Loizeaux Brothers, 1929.

Kent, Homer A., Jr., *Treasures of Wisdom: Studies in Colossians and Philemon*. Grand Rapids: Baker Book House, 1978.

Lightfoot, J. B. *St. Paul's Epistles to the Colossians and to Philemon*. Grand Rapids: Zondervan Publishing House, 1979.

Martin, Ralph P. *Colossians: The Church's Lord and the Christian's Liberty*. Grand Rapids: Zondervan Publishing House, 1975.

Moule, H. C. G. *Studies in Colossians and Philemon*. Grand Rapids: Kregel Publications, 1977.

Robertson, Archibald Thomas. *Word Pictures in the New Testament*. Vol. 4. Nashville: Broadman Press, 1931.

Simpson, E. K., and Bruce, Frederick F. *Commentary on the Epistles to Ephesians and Colossians*. Grand Rapids: Wm. B. Eerdmans Publishing Co., 1958.